Hyper-V 2016 Best Practices

Harness the power of Hyper-V 2016 to build high-performance infrastructures that suit your needs

Benedict Berger
Romain Serre

BIRMINGHAM - MUMBAI

Hyper-V 2016 Best Practices

First published: November 2014

Second edition: October 2016

Production reference: 1251016

Published by Packt Publishing Ltd.
Livery Place
35 Livery Street
Birmingham
B3 2PB, UK.
ISBN 978-1-78588-339-2

www.packtpub.com

Credits

Authors

Benedict Berger
Romain Serre

Reviewer

Romeo Mlinar

Commissioning Editor

Kartikey Pandey

Acquisition Editors

Juned Patel
Mansi Sanghavi

Content Development Editor

Mehvash Fatima

Technical Editor

Devesh Chugh

Copy Editor

Tom Jacob

Project Coordinator

Kinjal Bari

Proofreader

Safis Editing

Indexer

Pratik Shirodkar

Graphics

Kirk D'Penha

Production Coordinator

Deepika Naik

About the Authors

Benedict Berger was the author of the first edition of this book (*Hyper-V Best Practices* by *Packt Publishing*). He works as a technology solutions professional at Microsoft. He blogs on the German Virtualization Blog (`http://blogs.technet.com/b/germanvirtualizationbl og/`) and on his personal blog (`http://blog.benedict-berger.de`).

Romain Serre works in Lyon as a senior consultant. He is focused on Microsoft Technology, especially on Hyper-V, System Center, Storage, networking, and Cloud OS technology such as Microsoft Azure or Azure Stack. He is an MVP and a certified Microsoft Certified Solution Expert (MCSE Server Infrastructure and Private Cloud), on Hyper-V and on Microsoft Azure (implementing a Microsoft Azure solution). He blogs at `http://www.tech -coffee.net`.

About the Reviewer

Romeo Mlinar has been working as the head of the IT department at an IT company in Zagreb, Croatia. Professionally, he is connected with computer technology for more than a decade. He is passionately devoted to Microsoft products and technology, such as, System Center, Team Foundation Server, planning and design of Active Directory, as well as Windows Server services, devoting special attention to virtualization (Hyper-V), which is his recent preoccupation. He holds a large number of Microsoft industrial certifications, such as MCSA, MCSE, MCDST, MCTS, MCDBA, MCITP, MCS: Server Virtualization, MCSE: Private Cloud, MCSE: Server Infrastructure, and so on. Since 2012, he is a Microsoft Most Valuable Professional (MVP) for Cloud and Datacenter Management [Hyper-V]. He is a regular speaker at various IT conferences regionally and abroad. Also, he is an IT Pro User Group Zagreb lead. He spends his free time with people from the IT world, acquiring new knowledge, eagerly sharing it with others, while at the same time enjoying his life with his family. He blogs at `http://blog.mlinar.biz/`.

www.PacktPub.com

For support files and downloads related to your book, please visit www.PacktPub.com.

Did you know that Packt offers eBook versions of every book published, with PDF and ePub files available? You can upgrade to the eBook version at www.PacktPub.com and as a print book customer, you are entitled to a discount on the eBook copy. Get in touch with us at service@packtpub.com for more details.

At www.PacktPub.com, you can also read a collection of free technical articles, sign up for a range of free newsletters and receive exclusive discounts and offers on Packt books and eBooks.

https://www.packtpub.com/mapt

Get the most in-demand software skills with Mapt. Mapt gives you full access to all Packt books and video courses, as well as industry-leading tools to help you plan your personal development and advance your career.

Why subscribe?

- Fully searchable across every book published by Packt
- Copy and paste, print, and bookmark content
- On demand and accessible via a web browser

Table of Contents

Preface

Today we virtualize datacenters to gain flexibility, scalability, high-end performance, and ease of management. Moreover, virtualization has brought a high level of consolidation. This enables us to reduce the footprint of the datacenter and save power. For some years, we have wanted to manage our datacenter using the Cloud model. We wanted to create server quickly, improve the performance of this machine on the fly, and delete it when we don't need it anymore.

All of this can be done, thanks to hypervisor. There are several hypervisors such as VMware ESX, Citrix XenServer, or Microsoft Hyper-V. Because this book is called *Hyper-V Best Practices*, we will focus on Hyper-V.

Microsoft has released a major Windows Server version toward the end of 2016. This book focusses on Hyper-V on Windows Server 2016. A lot of new features have been provided in this new version but several rules can be applied to Hyper-V in a previous release.

This book is not intended to explain you all feature mechanisms included in Hyper-V. To follow this book, some knowledge of Hyper-V is required. However, because Hyper-V doesn't work alone, you also need to know about Failover Cluster, Active Directory, storage, and network.

Fasten your seat belts and welcome to this Hyper-V journey.

What this book covers

Chapter 1, *Accelerating Hyper-V Deployment*, gives you some tips to automate Hyper-V and VM deployment, because, in a huge environment, you may want to automate some tasks to limit human errors and to save time.

Chapter 2, *Deploying Highly Available Hyper-V Clusters*, teaches you how to deploy a Hyper-V cluster and how to leverage it to keep your application working, because, in production, you usually want high availability to keep the application working even in cases of incidents.

Chapter 3, *Backup and Disaster Recovery*, describes how to leverage Windows Server 2016 and Microsoft Azure to back up your workloads and to failover in another room in case of a disaster because companies want to always back up their workloads and make a Disaster Recovery Plan in case a datacenter is out of order.

Chapter 4, *Storage Best Practices*, introduces some best practices to leverage the best of your underlying storage system because the storage is a significant piece in a virtual environment. Without good storage, you can expect poor performance.

Chapter 5, *Network Best Practices*, describes some best practices about the network and Hyper-V, because, similar to the storage, the network is a masterpiece for your virtual environment, especially when implementing a software-defined storage system.

Chapter 6, *Highly Effective Hyper-V Design*, will help you to choose a design for your Hyper-V infrastructure depending on the performance you want and the budget you have.

Chapter 7, *Hyper-V Performance Tuning*, will help you to reach the performance you expect.

Chapter 8, *Management with System Center and Azure*, introduces System Center and Microsoft Azure features which work well with Hyper-V because Microsoft has a big ecosystem that can interact with Hyper-V.

Chapter 9, *Migration to Hyper-V 2016*, will help you to achieve the migration if you are still in Windows Server 2012 R2 or VMware and you want to migrate to Hyper-V 2016.

What you need for this book

This book describes the best practices about Hyper-V included in Windows Server 2016. So all the screenshots, PowerShell cmdlets, and XML files have been tested on this Windows Server version. To follow the indication of this book you need Windows Server 2016.

Moreover, some chapters describe System Center and some features provided by Microsoft Azure. To follow all chapters, you need an Azure subscription and System Center 2016.

Other tools that are introduced are free. So you can easily download them from the Internet.

Who this book is for

If you are working with Hyper-V and want to optimize its performance and effectiveness, this book is for you. This book will help you close the gap between the Hyper-V lab and production environments.

Conventions

In this book, you will find a number of styles of text that distinguish between different kinds of information. Here are some examples of these styles, and an explanation of their meaning.

Code words in text, database table names, folder names, filenames, file extensions, pathnames, dummy URLs, user input, and Twitter handles are shown as follows: Code words in text are shown as follows: "The unattended setup uses configurations saved in a precreated `unattended.xml` file."

A PowerShell cmdlet is set as follows:

```
New-VM -Name VM01 -Generation 2
```

An XML file is set as follows:

```xml
<?xml version="1.0" encoding="UTF-8"?>
<component name="Microsoft-Windows-International-Core-
WinPE" processorArchitecture="amd64" publicKeyToken="31bf3856ad364e35"
language="neutral" versionScope="nonSxS"
xmlns:wcm="http://schemas.microsoft.com/WMIConfig/2002/Sta
te" xmlns:xsi="http://www.w3.org/2001/XMLSchema-instance">
  <SetupUILanguage>
     <UILanguage>en-US</UILanguage>
  </SetupUILanguage>
  <InputLocale>en-US</InputLocale>
  <UILanguage>en-US</UILanguage>
  <SystemLocale>en-US</SystemLocale>
  <UserLocale>en-US</UserLocale>
</component>
```

New terms and important words are shown in bold. Words that you see on the screen, in menus or dialog boxes for example, appear in the text like this: "Start the setup of the Windows ADK you downloaded earlier. At the setup prompt, select only **Deployment Tools**".

 Warnings or important notes appear in a box like this.

 Tips and tricks appear like this.

Reader feedback

Feedback from our readers is always welcome. Let us know what you think about this book—what you liked or disliked. Reader feedback is important for us as it helps us develop titles that you will really get the most out of. To send us general feedback, simply e-mail feedback@packtpub.com, and mention the book's title in the subject of your message. If there is a topic that you have expertise in and you are interested in either writing or contributing to a book, see our author guide at www.packtpub.com/authors.

Customer support

Now that you are the proud owner of a Packt book, we have a number of things to help you to get the most from your purchase.

Downloading the example code

You can download the example code files for this book from your account at http://www.packtpub.com. If you purchased this book elsewhere, you can visit http://www.packtpub.com/support and register to have the files e-mailed directly to you.

You can download the code files by following these steps:

1. Log in or register to our website using your e-mail address and password.
2. Hover the mouse pointer on the **SUPPORT** tab at the top.
3. Click on **Code Downloads & Errata**.
4. Enter the name of the book in the **Search** box.
5. Select the book for which you're looking to download the code files.
6. Choose from the drop-down menu where you purchased this book from.
7. Click on **Code Download**.

Once the file is downloaded, please make sure that you unzip or extract the folder using the latest version of:

- WinRAR / 7-Zip for Windows
- Zipeg / iZip / UnRarX for Mac
- 7-Zip / PeaZip for Linux

The code bundle for the book is also hosted on GitHub at `https://github.com/Hyper-V-2 016-Best-Practices/`. We also have other code bundles from our rich catalog of books and videos available at `https://github.com/PacktPublishing/`. Check them out!

Downloading the color images of this book

We also provide you with a PDF file that has color images of the screenshots/diagrams used in this book. The color images will help you better understand the changes in the output. You can download this file from `http://www.packtpub.com/sites/default/files/downl oads/HyperV2016BestPractices_ColorImages.pdf`.

Errata

Although we have taken every care to ensure the accuracy of our content, mistakes do happen. If you find a mistake in one of our books—maybe a mistake in the text or the code—we would be grateful if you could report this to us. By doing so, you can save other readers from frustration and help us improve subsequent versions of this book. If you find any errata, please report them by visiting `http://www.packtpub.com/submit-errata`, selecting your book, clicking on the **Errata Submission Form** link, and entering the details of your errata. Once your errata are verified, your submission will be accepted and the errata will be uploaded to our website or added to any list of existing errata under the Errata section of that title.

To view the previously submitted errata, go to `https://www.packtpub.com/books/content/support` and enter the name of the book in the search field. The required information will appear under the **Errata** section.

Piracy

Piracy of copyrighted material on the Internet is an ongoing problem across all media. At Packt, we take the protection of our copyright and licenses very seriously. If you come across any illegal copies of our works in any form on the Internet, please provide us with the location address or website name immediately so that we can pursue a remedy.

Please contact us at `copyright@packtpub.com` with a link to the suspected pirated material.

We appreciate your help in protecting our authors and our ability to bring you valuable content.

Questions

If you have a problem with any aspect of this book, you can contact us at `questions@packtpub.com`, and we will do our best to address the problem.

1
Accelerating Hyper-V Deployment

"Based on my slogan 'Keep It Smart and Simple (K.I.S.S.),' the planning phase is essential for a successful implementation of a Hyper-V environment."
Andreas Baumgarten – MVP System Center Cloud and Datacenter Management

This chapter provides an overview of how to automate the installation of the best practice Hyper-V host and its first running **virtual machines** (**VMs**). You will learn how to create unattended installations of Hyper-V with minimal effort. All the examples shown in this chapter are proven real-world best practice ones.

This chapter includes the following topics:

- Planning the Hyper-V host
- Unattended installation of Hyper-V through XML files
- Rapid deployment of virtual machines
- Nano Server

Why Hyper-V projects fail

Before you start deploying your first production Hyper-V host, make sure that you have completed a detailed planning phase. I have been called in to many Hyper-V projects to assist in repairing what a *specialist* has implemented. Most of the time, I start by correcting the design because the biggest failures happen there, but are only discovered later, during implementation. I remember many projects in which I was called in to assist with installations and configurations during the implementation phases, because these were the project phases where a real expert was needed.

However, based on experience, this notion is wrong. Most critical to a successful design phase are two features-its rare existence and someone with technological and organizational experience with Hyper-V. If you don't have the latter, look out for a Microsoft Partner with a Gold Competency called **Management and Virtualization** on Microsoft Pinpoint (`http://pinpoint.microsoft.com`) and take a quick look at the reviews given by customers for successful Hyper-V projects.

 If you think it's expensive to hire a professional, wait until you hire an amateur. Having an expert in the design phase is the best way to accelerate your Hyper-V project.

Before you start your first deployment in production, make sure you have defined the aim of the project and its smart criteria and have done a thorough analysis of the current state. After this, you should be able to plan the necessary steps to reach the target state, including a pilot phase.

Planning your environment

Besides the organizational skill needed for a successful Hyper-V project, there are some helpful tools that can help in most cases with the technical details. For answering questions such as how many hosts I will need for my Hyper-V setup, how many CPUs and how much RAM is needed, and what bandwidth is needed on my network, I commonly use the free Solution Accelerator, **Microsoft Assessment and Planning Toolkit (MAP Toolkit)** by Microsoft (downloadable at the shortlink `http://bit.ly/1lzt2mJ`). The MAP Toolkit is shown in the following screenshot:

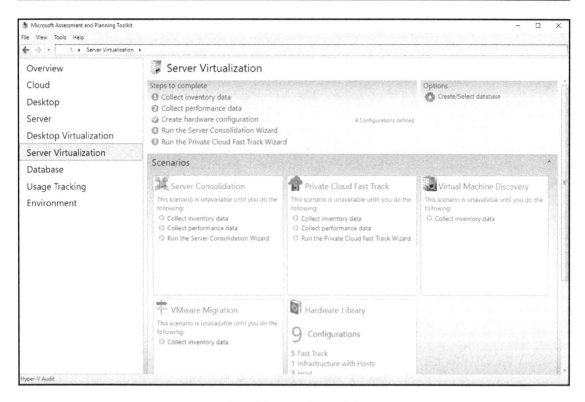

Microsoft Assessment and Planning Tools

The easy-to-use MAP Toolkit does a full inventory of your existing environment, including performance counters over time. After running the wizards in your existing infrastructure, you will get an overview, a detailed report of the existing hardware and software infrastructure, and- most importantly -a measure of how these are used in your datacenter as of today, including used CPU cycles, memory, Storage I/O, and network usage. MAP even includes a planning wizard to plan the hardware requirements of your future Hyper-V hosts based on your current workloads and hardware configurations.

After having a basic understanding of the current usage and future needs of your hardware, it's time to choose the appropriate servers to run Hyper-V and its VMs. The good news is that all major server vendors have hardware in their portfolio that performs well for this task, so choose whatever vendor you like; there is just one thing you absolutely need to make sure of. The chosen hardware should be on the Windows Server Catalog and be certified for Windows Server 2016 (you can get more information here `http://bit.ly/29W93Mg`). This way, you are making sure that your hardware has undergone extensive testing for Windows Server 2016 with Hyper-V. You will be able to open a support call at Microsoft in case you ever run into problems using this hardware with Hyper-V. If you are going to use an older version of Hyper-V (which you should avoid, but licenses might force you to), select the corresponding host OS on the hardware catalog. Make sure that your host setup includes the necessary adapters to comply with your chosen storage (refer to `Chapter 4`, *Storage Best Practices*) and network designs (refer to `Chapter 5`, *Network Best Practices*).

The CPU vendor you choose won't make a huge difference; just make sure that you stick to one, because mixed CPU vendors won't allow you to use live migration between Hyper-V hosts. Be sure that the chosen CPU models have support for server virtualization (Intel VT/AMD-V) and Data Execution Prevention (XD/NX) enabled. I strongly recommend that you use hyperthreading-enabled CPUs for server virtualization with active **Second Level Address Translation** (**SLAT**). Both are hardware-accelerated CPU features that add more performance to Hyper-V. For best performance, make sure to buy CPU models from the newest certified Enterprise Server line of the vendor of your choice. Due to the current licensing of Windows Server 2016 Datacenter and several other products, I recommend that you choose CPUs to obtain at least 16 physical cores in a server. If you need more physical cores, you have to buy extra license packs for every two additional physical cores in the server.

To choose the right RAM for your Hyper-V hosts, make sure that it supports the **Error Checking and Correction** (**ECC**) RAM and choose modules large enough to fit with the amount designed into your hosts. As RAM is very inexpensive these days, you should choose the bigger modules in case of any doubts on ensuring growth in future.

For your storage and networking options, refer to the corresponding chapters of this book. However, to host the Hyper-V management partition, I strongly recommend that you use two local SSDs or HDDs in Raid 1 and not share the disks with VMs or other data. I have experienced the best results with these local hard drives, and have found some problems with remote boot scenarios due to the higher complexity of boot-from-SAN setups, which is also a possible and supported, but not a preferred scenario. You don't need high-performance disks for the OS; all I/O performance should be added to the VM storage.

It is also important to choose fewer bigger boxes over many small Hyper-V hosts. This enables more efficient management. However, while needing a failover resource in a cluster, a Hyper-V cluster should consist of at least three nodes; otherwise, 50 percent of your hardware is reserved for failover scenarios.

Refer to `Chapter 7`, *Hyper-V Performance Tuning*; it includes advanced hardware sizing guidelines for performance tuning.

Preparing your host systems

Many *Prepare Your System* chapters start by asking you to update all your hardware and software components to the latest releases. This chapter doesn't make an exception to this rule. In no other technical area have I seen so many successfully fixed environments due to firmware and driver updates. Windows Server with Hyper-V has undergone a very rapid development cycle with many releases in a short timeframe. Most hardware vendors released firmware and drivers with greatly shortened testing periods and were forced to release several updates due to firmware and driver updates to their products. Before you start setting up your Hyper-V host, update BIOS, RAID Controller, and the **Network Interface Card** (**NIC**) firmware to their latest release. Use the home page of the server-vendor, not the vendor of the individual components, for reference to the latest certified releases. Only use downloads from the individual component's' vendor if you see those problems you encounter fixed by the corresponding release notes.

A Hyper-V host is highly dependent on the underlying hardware. Be very careful with the implementation; try and test every hardware component, every driver and firmware. Do not add in the production before double checking every single part of your newly created Hyper-V host. Moreover, use only supported driver and firmware.

Other than this, you only need your Hyper-V installation media, the Windows 10 **Assessment and Deployment Kit** (**ADK**) (shortlink `http://bit.ly/29Ub3G5`), and a USB drive to prepare for rapid Hyper-V installations. Download either the full version of Windows Server 2016 with Hyper-V from your Volume License Portal or the 180-day Evaluation version of Hyper-V. In fact, it does not make any difference whether you use the Evaluation edition or the full version media- they are interchangeable -the only difference will be made by the product key you enter. All Hyper-V features are also supported by the free editions of Hyper-V Server 2016; all the screenshots and configurations you see in this book are created using the full version of Windows Server 2016 with Hyper-V and could vary slightly from the free edition. Hyper-V is very easy to install.

Windows Server 2016 comes with a new licensing model based on core. Microsoft sells the license pack to support two cores. You need to buy at least eight license packs that support 16 cores. If you have beyond 16 cores in the server, you will have to buy extra license packs. In the following table, you can find the features provided by each edition:

Feature Differentiation: Datacenter and Standard Editions		
Feature	**Datacenter Edition**	**Standard Edition**
Core functionality of Windows Server	●	●
OSEs / Hyper-V Containers	Unlimited	2
Windows Server containers	Unlimited	Unlimited
Host Guardian Service	●	●
Nano Server*	●	●
Storage features including Storage Spaces Direct and Storage Replica	●	
Shielded Virtual Machines	●	
Networking stack	●	

Comparison between both Windows server editions

To familiarize yourself with Hyper-V, just insert the installation media, select it as the boot device, and click through the various options in the setup wizard. If this will be the only Hyper-V host you will ever install, this will be a great installation experience. Most of the time you will not stick to just one host and, to speed things up, we will mainly use unattended installations of the Hyper-V hosts from now on. The unattended setup uses configurations saved in a precreated `unattended.xml` file, which can be either slipstreamed into the installation media or saved on a USB drive so that it's available to the host during installation. This enables a standardized and very rapid Hyper-V deployment with a onetime preparation.

About Nano Server

Nano Server is a new headless installation option in Windows Server 2016. Nano Server is similar to Windows Server in the server core mode, but without logon capabilities and the support of only 64-bit applications, tools, and agent. It provides a small OS footprint, a quick restart, and a far fewer updates. Since there is no GUI and no logon capabilities on Nano Server, the management is made remotely using PowerShell, WinRM, WMI or MMC. To run Nano Server in production, you need the Software Assurance. Nano Server (shortlink `http://bit.ly/2acV3Q2`) supports a lot of features such as Hyper-V, Failover Cluster, storage, and so on.

However, the servicing model provided with Nano Server requires a lot of build upgrade in a year. Nano Server follows the same servicing model as Windows 10 in enterprise called **Current Branch for Business (CBB)**. CBB should be updated at least twice a year and it will be applied to Nano Server. These updates must be activated manually but Microsoft supports only the current branch and its immediate predecessor.

Because of the CBB servicing model, I do not recommend that you use Nano Server in production for Hyper-V and storage features. These features require efficiency and stability and need to be operational as long as possible. This is the exact opposite of what is provided by the CBB servicing model.

Creating unattended installation files

To create an `unattended.xml` file, you can either start from scratch with a simple text editor or use a GUI. To leverage the second option, follow these steps:

1. Start the setup of the Windows ADK you downloaded earlier. At the setup prompt, select only **Deployment Tools**, as shown in the following screenshot.

2. After the completion of the installation, start **Windows System Image Manager** from the **Start** screen:

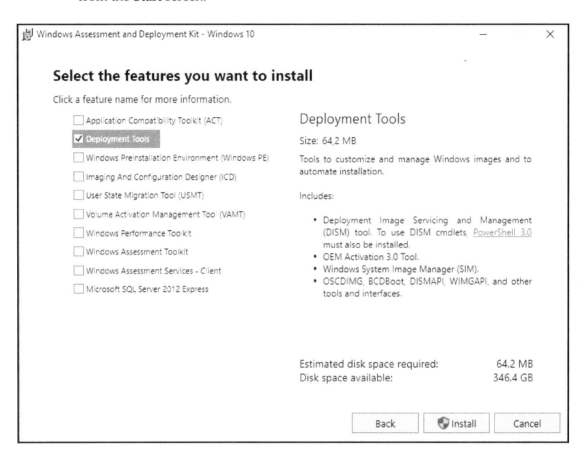

Windows ADK 10

3. After the tool is fully loaded, select the **File** menu, open the **Select an Image** wizard, and browse to the `Install.wim` file or your installation media in the source's subdirectory.

4. Select the **Windows Server 2016 SERVER STANDARD** edition for your first unattended installation file and allow the creation of a new catalog file:

   - If you receive a warning message stating that you are unable to write the catalog file, open Windows Explorer, navigate to the `Install.wim` file, open its properties, and uncheck the **read only** checkbox

- If you have your installation media on a physical read-only media, copy `Install.wim` to a local hard drive first. Select the Server Standard Edition using GUI:

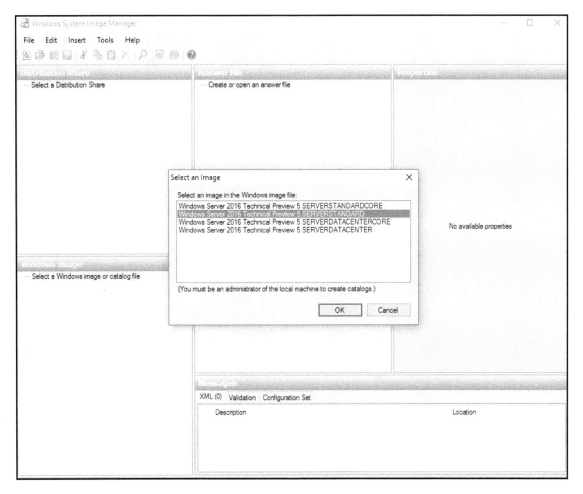

Select Windows Edition

5. After the catalog file is created, select the **File** menu again, create a **New Answer File**, and save it as `unattended.xml` to a place of your choice.

6. **Windows System Image Manager** will then create the basic XML structure of your unattended file, as shown in the following screenshot:

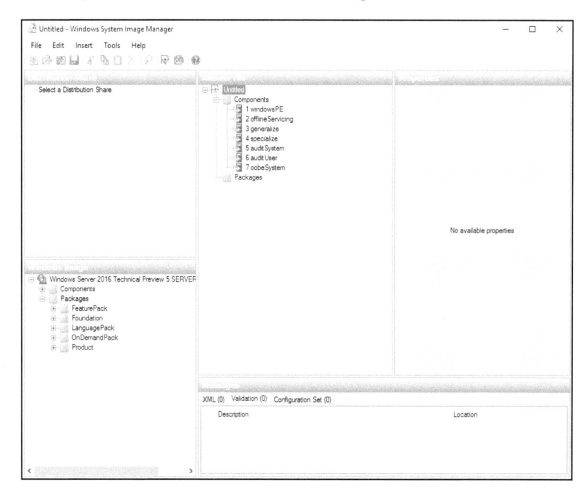

Windows System Image Manager

7. Opening this XML file in Internet Explorer will show you the actual file contents. Every Windows Server 2016 setup will check for an existing `unattended.xml` file at the start of every available drive letter, but it will only work if the XML structure is correct.

8. We will now continue to fill this `unattended.xml` file with contents specific to the Hyper-V setup to allow a Zero-Touch installation of your Hyper-V hosts.

Adding basic components

Start by adding the most basic components by expanding the Components tree under the **Windows Image** section in the left-hand corner of the tool. Let's now add language and locale information, through following steps:

1. First, add the `amd64_Microsoft-Windows-International-Core-WinPE` components to `Pass1` and fill the basic language options. The generated XML part with all the mandatory parameters will look like the following code:

```xml
<?xml version="1.0" encoding="UTF-8"?>
<component name="Microsoft-Windows-International-Core-WinPE"
processorArchitecture="amd64" publicKeyToken="31bf3856ad364e35"
language="neutral" versionScope="nonSxS"
xmlns:wcm="http://schemas.microsoft.com/WMIConfig/2002/State"
xmlns:xsi="http://www.w3.org/2001/XMLSchema-instance">
        <SetupUILanguage>
            <UILanguage>en-US</UILanguage>
        </SetupUILanguage>
        <InputLocale>en-US</InputLocale>
        <UILanguage>en-US</UILanguage>
        <SystemLocale>en-US</SystemLocale>
        <UserLocale>en-US</UserLocale>
    </component>
```

   If you prefer language settings other than US English, make sure that the language components are included in the installation media and refer to the correct locale IDs, which can be found on Microsoft MSDN (shortlink `http://bit.ly/1gMNu2B`).

2. Next, add `amd64_Microsoft-Windows-Setup_neutral` to `Pass1` to configure some basic OS configurations such as Disk Layout. A generated sample XML part for a BIOS-based system is as follows:

```xml
<?xml version="1.0" encoding="UTF-8"?>
<component name="Microsoft-Windows-Setup" processorArchitecture="amd64"
publicKeyToken="31bf3856ad364e35" language="neutral" versionScope="nonSxS"
xmlns:wcm="http://schemas.microsoft.com/WMIConfig/2002/State"
xmlns:xsi="http://www.w3.org/2001/XMLSchema-instance">
  <DiskConfiguration>
    <Disk wcm:action="add">
      <CreatePartitions>
        <CreatePartition wcm:action="add">
          <Order>1</Order>
          <Size>350</Size>
          <Type>Primary</Type>
```

```
      </CreatePartition>
      <CreatePartition wcm:action="add">
        <Order>2</Order>
        <Extend>true</Extend>
        <Type>Primary</Type>
      </CreatePartition>
    </CreatePartitions>
    <ModifyPartitions>
      <ModifyPartition wcm:action="add">
        <Active>true</Active>
        <Format>NTFS</Format>
        <Label>Bitlocker</Label>
        <Order>1</Order>
        <PartitionID>1</PartitionID>
      </ModifyPartition>
      <ModifyPartition wcm:action="add">
        <Letter>C</Letter>
        <Label>HostOS</Label>
        <Order>2</Order>
        <PartitionID>2</PartitionID>
      </ModifyPartition>
    </ModifyPartitions>
    <DiskID>0</DiskID>
    <WillWipeDisk>true</WillWipeDisk>
  </Disk>
  </DiskConfiguration>
</component>
```

This configuration will make sure that there are clean partitions that follow Microsoft's default deployment model. The small partition at the start of the disk is created to support Bitlocker. Microsoft's full disk encryption can be used with Hyper-V hosts and can also be activated later. The use of Bitlocker is only recommended in high-security environments.

3. If your host does not have BIOS anymore and uses an UEFI-based setup routine, the XML file will be edited to include the following code as well:

```
<?xml version="1.0" encoding="UTF-8"?>
<component name="Microsoft-Windows-Setup" processorArchitecture="amd64"
publicKeyToken="31bf3856ad364e35" language="neutral" versionScope="nonSxS"
xmlns:wcm="http://schemas.microsoft.com/WMIConfig/2002/State"
xmlns:xsi="http://www.w3.org/2001/XMLSchema-instance">
  <DiskConfiguration>
    <Disk wcm:action="add">
      <CreatePartitions>
        <CreatePartition wcm:action="add">
          <Order>2</Order>
```

```
            <Size>100</Size>
            <Type>EFI</Type>
          </CreatePartition>
          <CreatePartition wcm:action="add">
            <Order>3</Order>
            <Extend>false</Extend>
            <Type>MSR</Type>
            <Size>128</Size>
          </CreatePartition>
          <CreatePartition wcm:action="add">
            <Order>4</Order>
            <Extend>true</Extend>
            <Type>Primary</Type>
          </CreatePartition>
          <CreatePartition wcm:action="add">
            <Size>350</Size>
            <Type>Primary</Type>
            <Order>1</Order>
          </CreatePartition>
        </CreatePartitions>
        <ModifyPartitions>
          <ModifyPartition wcm:action="add">
            <Active>false</Active>
            <Format>NTFS</Format>
            <Label>Bitlocker</Label>
            <Order>1</Order>
            <PartitionID>1</PartitionID>
          </ModifyPartition>
          <ModifyPartition wcm:action="add">
            <Letter>C</Letter>
            <Label>HostOS</Label>
            <Order>3</Order>
            <PartitionID>3</PartitionID>
            <Format>NTFS</Format>
          </ModifyPartition>
          <ModifyPartition wcm:action="add">
            <Order>2</Order>
            <PartitionID>2</PartitionID>
            <Label>EFI</Label>
            <Format>FAT32</Format>
            <Active>false</Active>
          </ModifyPartition>
        </ModifyPartitions>
        <DiskID>0</DiskID>
        <WillWipeDisk>true</WillWipeDisk>
      </Disk>
    </DiskConfiguration>
  </component>
```

Which edition to install

In Windows Server 2012 R2, the Standard and the Datacenter editions have exactly the same features. The main difference between the Standard and Datacenter editions is the virtualization rights. Each Windows Server Standard edition allows you to run two guest **Operating System Environments** (**OSEs**) with Windows Server editions, and a Datacenter edition allows you to run an unlimited number of Windows Server VMs on this particular licensed Hyper-V host. There is only one technical difference between the two editions-on a Datacenter edition, all Windows Server guest VMs will be automatically activated when provided with a corresponding key during setup. There is no need for a MAK or KMS-based OS activation anymore.

With Windows Server 2016, some features are not present in the Standard edition compared to the Datacenter edition. The mainly missing features in the Standard edition are related to Storage (as Storage Spaces Direct), networking stack, and Shield VMs. As of Windows Server 2012 R2, the Datacenter edition allows you to run unlimited guest OSEs (or Hyper-V containers) while the Standard edition allows you to run two of them.

If you want to leverage **Automatic Virtual Machine Activation** (**AVMA**), storage features, and unlimited number of Windows Server VMs, install a Datacenter edition on the host. It is easy to upgrade a Standard edition to a Datacenter edition later, but there is no option to downgrade.

If you are not sure which edition you are using, open a PowerShell window with administrative privileges and run the following command:

```
get-windowsedition -online
```

To find out which editions are available for upgrade, run the following command:

```
Get-WindowsEdition -online -target
```

Finally, to upgrade to the target edition, run the following command:

```
dism.exe /online /Set-Edition:ServerDatacenterCor /AcceptEula
/ProductKey:   <ProductKey>
```

```
PS C:\Users\Administrator> dism.exe /online /Set-Edition:ServerDatacenterCor /AcceptEula /ProductKey:


Deployment Image Servicing and Management tool
Version: 10.0.14300.1000

Image Version: 10.0.14300.1000

Starting to update components...
Starting to install product key...
Finished installing product key.

Removing package Microsoft-Windows-ServerStandardEvalCorEdition~31bf3856ad364e35~amd64~~10.0.14300.1000
[==========================100.0%==========================]
Finished updating components.

Starting to apply edition-specific settings...
Finished applying edition-specific settings.

The operation completed successfully.
Restart Windows to complete this operation.
Do you want to restart the computer now? (Y/N)
```

Upgrade from the Standard edition to the Datacenter edition

While it's suitable to install a Datacenter edition on a Hyper-V host, you should never do this inside a virtual machine, except if you need specific features only available in the Datacenter edition. For example, if you want to make a virtual Storage Spaces Direct lab, you need the Datacenter edition to deploy this feature. In most environment, the Datacenter edition is deployed because it enables you to run unlimited guest OSes while the Standard edition enables you to run just two guest OSes. The next step in building our unattended installation is to set up the installation target and the edition. Navigate to the `ImageInstall` string under the `Microsoft-Windows-Setup` node and add the following code:

```
<ImageInstall><OSImage><InstallFrom><MetaData
wcm:action="add"><Key>/Image/Name</Key><Value>Windows Server 2016 Technical
Preview 5
SERVERSTANDARD</Value></MetaData></InstallFrom><InstallTo><DiskID>0</DiskID
><PartitionID>2</PartitionID></InstallTo></OSImage></ImageInstall>
```

If you have chosen the UEFI-based setup, choose `PartitionID 4` according to your disk setup. This will make sure that you install the Standard edition of Windows Server 2016 to the correct partition.

As the last step in `Pass1`, we will fill out the `UserData` tree under the `Microsoft-Windows-Setup` node and edit the following code:

```
<UserData><ProductKey><WillShowUI>OnError</WillShowUI></ProductKey><AcceptE
ula>true</AcceptEula><FullName>YourName</FullName><Organization>YourOrg</Or
ganization></UserData>
```

Fill in **Name** and **Org Data** with anything you like; however, these fields are mandatory. The **product key** field is optional. If you intend to use a 180-day trial version of Windows Server or are leveraging KMS Server activation capabilities, do not enter a product key. If you are using MAK-based OS activations, enter your product key. You can also install a MAK product key at a later time by opening a PowerShell window with administrative privileges and running the following command:

```
slmgr -upk #(this uninstalls the current product key)
slmgr -ipk <key> #(including dashes)
```

Decide whether to GUI

After adding the basic parameters, it's now time to add some comfort to our Zero-Touch installation.

In **Windows System Image Manager**, add `amd64_Microsoft-Windows-Shell-Setup_neutral` to `Pass4` and `Pass7`.

Edit the XML file to set your time zone settings (run `tzutil /l` in a Shell to get a list of all the valid time zones) and your local administrator password. Don't worry about entering a password into **Windows System Image Manager**; it will encrypt the password while saving the file. The following code shows how to set the regional and user information:

```
<settings pass="specialize"><component language="neutral"
xmlns:xsi="http://www.w3.org/2001/XMLSchema-instance"
xmlns:wcm="http://schemas.microsoft.com/WMIConfig/2002/State"
versionScope="nonSxS" publicKeyToken="31bf3856ad364e35"
processorArchitecture="amd64" name="Microsoft-Windows-Shell-
Setup"><TimeZone>W. Europe Standard
Time</TimeZone></component></settings><settings
pass="oobeSystem"><component language="neutral"
xmlns:xsi="http://www.w3.org/2001/XMLSchema-instance"
xmlns:wcm="http://schemas.microsoft.com/WMIConfig/2002/State"
versionScope="nonSxS" publicKeyToken="31bf3856ad364e35"
processorArchitecture="amd64" name="Microsoft-Windows-Shell-
Setup"><UserAccounts><AdministratorPassword><Value>UABAAHMAcwB3ADAAcgBkAEEA
ZABtAGkAbgBpAHMAdAByAGEAdABvAHIAUABhAHMAcwB3AG8AcgBkAA==</Value><PlainText>
false</PlainText></AdministratorPassword></UserAccounts></component></setti
ngs>
```

To allow a rapid deployment of hosts, I have not entered a computer name at this stage, so the setup will generate a random computer name for each node installed. If you want to enter a computer name, add the following code to your XML-specialized section:

```
<ComputerName>Hyper-V01</ComputerName>
```

 Downloading the example code:
You can download the example code files for all Packt books you have purchased from your account at http://www.packtpub.com. If you purchased this book elsewhere, you can visit http://www.packtpub.com/support and register to have the files e-mailed directly to you.

Another optional feature was selected right at the beginning of our XML creation-the GUI. By selecting the Windows Server Standard edition and not the Standard Core edition, we have included the complete GUI of Windows Server in our setup. Unlike Windows Server 2012 R2 version with Hyper-V, the GUI is now a feature that can't be activated or deactivated at a later stage. Note that the GUI is not available on the free Hyper-V Server 2016. The full GUI installation process offers the same great user experience we know from many versions of Windows Server and Windows Client operating systems, but Server Core is the installation method recommended by Microsoft for Windows Server 2016 and Hyper-V. The Core installation option offers a reduced attack surface with less patching efforts and fewer reboots. It even comes with a smaller resource footprint than its Full GUI equivalent. However, offering only a PowerShell Window as the single point of local administration discouraged many system administrators in the past, so Core setups aren't found often. Don't forget that all administrative APIs are active on a Core Server, so you can connect with your MMC consoles from other servers or clients without the need to use the PowerShell modules. Unfortunately, in Windows Server 2016 you can't switch from GUI installation to Core installation or vice versa.

The Minshell is also no longer available. In Windows Server 2012 R2, Minshell was a deployment option similar to the Core installation option but with **Remote Server Administration Tools (RSAT)**.

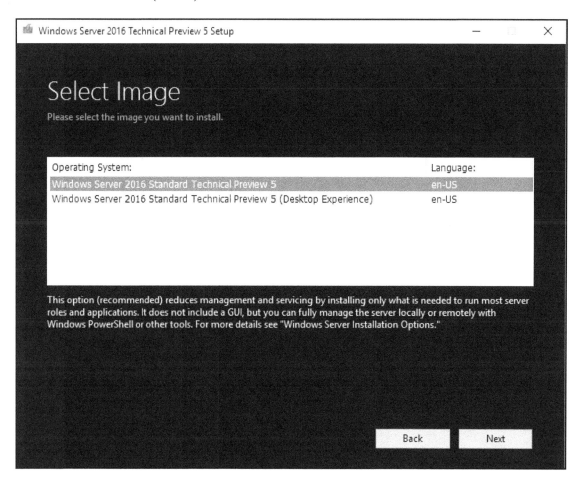

GUI or Core installation

Hyper-V hosts in Active Directory domains

The basic operating system setup will now already be based on a Zero-Touch installation, but we want to achieve more than this and will include some additional options.

Add the `amd64_Microsoft-Windows-TerminalServices-LocalSessionManager` component to `Pass4` and configure it to enable Remote Desktop Access to the server:

```xml
<?xml version="1.0" encoding="UTF-8"?>
<component xmlns:wcm="http://schemas.microsoft.com/WMIConfig/2002/State"
xmlns:xsi="http://www.w3.org/2001/XMLSchema-instance" language="neutral"
versionScope="nonSxS" publicKeyToken="31bf3856ad364e35"
processorArchitecture="amd64" name="Microsoft-Windows-TerminalServices-
LocalSessionManager">
  <fDenyTSConnections>false</fDenyTSConnections>
</component>
```

To reach the Server via RDP, via its designated IP address, we will also set the basic network settings. Keep in mind that based on your converged network setup for Hyper-V, these might be overwritten at a later step (`Chapter 5`, *Network Best Practices*).

Add the `amd64_Microsoft-Windows-TCPIP` component to `Pass4` and configure a static IP Address-in this case, based on the name of the interface. This is also possible using the MAC address. Configure the network as shown in the following code:

```xml
<?xml version="1.0" encoding="UTF-8"?>
<component xmlns:wcm="http://schemas.microsoft.com/WMIConfig/2002/State"
xmlns:xsi="http://www.w3.org/2001/XMLSchema-instance" language="neutral"
versionScope="nonSxS" publicKeyToken="31bf3856ad364e35"
processorArchitecture="amd64" name="Microsoft-Windows-TCPIP">
  <Interfaces>
    <Interface wcm:action="add">
      <Ipv4Settings>
        <DhcpEnabled>false</DhcpEnabled>
        <Metric>10</Metric>
        <RouterDiscoveryEnabled>true</RouterDiscoveryEnabled>
      </Ipv4Settings>
      <UnicastIpAddresses>
        <IpAddress wcm:action="add"
wcm:keyValue="1">192.168.1.41/24</IpAddress>
      </UnicastIpAddresses>
      <Identifier>Local Area Connection</Identifier>
    </Interface>
  </Interfaces>
</component>
```

Whether Hyper-V hosts should be added to an Active Directory domain is a topic that is often discussed. Having seen a lot of Hyper-V environments, either domain-joined or workgroup-joined, my answer to this is a strong yes. Windows Server 2016 Servers can boot up even clusters when domain-joined without an Active Directory domain controller available, so this chicken-or-egg problem from earlier Hyper-V versions is not a problem anymore. Hyper-V will run without an Active Directory domain; however, very basic capabilities such as live migration won't be available on workgroup environments. Huge Hyper-V installations or high-security companies even leverage their own management domain to place their Hyper-V hosts into an Active Directory domain.

There is little security consideration standing against a huge management benefit, through credential management, group policies, and so on, so you should domain-join all Hyper-V hosts to your existing Active Directory domain. If your Hyper-V hosts will be placed in high-security environments, join them to a dedicated management domain (within a separated Active Directory forest) and not to your production domain.

Add the `amd64_Microsoft-Windows-UnattendedJoin` component to `Pass4` and configure it to join an existing Active Directory domain:

```
<?xml version="1.0" encoding="UTF-8"?>
<component xmlns:wcm="http://schemas.microsoft.com/WMIConfig/2002/State"
xmlns:xsi="http://www.w3.org/2001/XMLSchema-instance" language="neutral"
versionScope="nonSxS" publicKeyToken="31bf3856ad364e35"
processorArchitecture="amd64" name="Microsoft-Windows-UnattendedJoin">
  <Identification>
    <Credentials>
      <Domain>int.homecloud.net</Domain>
      <Password>Hannover96</Password>
      <Username>joindomain</Username>
    </Credentials>
    <JoinDomain>int.homecloud.net</JoinDomain>
    <MachineObjectOU>OU=Hyper-
    V,DC=int,DC=homecloud,DC=net</MachineObjectOU>
  </Identification>
</component>
```

A typical configuration that is seen in this step is the disabling of the Windows Firewall. In my opinion, this is a bad practice. The Windows Firewall is a great layer of security and should be configured to your needs, but not disabled. For a central Firewall configuration, we'll use Group Policy settings, so we don't need to include any configuration in our `unattended.xml`.

Activating Hyper-V features

After our operating system is prepared to host Hyper-V, it's time to activate the Hyper-V components. Add the following product packages and their roles and features to your `unattended.xml` file:

```
<?xml version="1.0" encoding="UTF-8"?>
<servicing>
  <package action="configure">
    <assemblyIdentity language="" publicKeyToken="31bf3856ad364e35"
    processorArchitecture="amd64" name="Microsoft-Windows-
    ServerStandardEdition" version="6.3.9600.16384" />
    <selection name="Microsoft-Hyper-V-Common-Drivers-Package"
    state="true" />
    <selection name="Microsoft-Hyper-V-Guest-Integration-Drivers-
    Package" state="true" />
    <selection name="Microsoft-Hyper-V-Server-Drivers-Package"
    state="true" />
    <selection name="Microsoft-Hyper-V-ServerEdition-Package"
    state="true" />
  </package>
  <package action="configure">
    <assemblyIdentity language="" publicKeyToken="31bf3856ad364e35"
    processorArchitecture="amd64" name="Microsoft-Windows-ServerCore-
    Package" version="6.3.9600.16384" />
    <selection name="Microsoft-Hyper-V" state="true" />
    <selection name="Microsoft-Hyper-V-Offline" state="true" />
    <selection name="Microsoft-Hyper-V-Online" state="true" />
    <selection name="VmHostAgent" state="true" />
    <selection name="AdminUI" state="true" />
    <selection name="ServerManager-Core-RSAT" state="true" />
    <selection name="ServerManager-Core-RSAT-Feature-Tools"
    state="true" />
    <selection name="ServerManager-Core-RSAT-Role-Tools" state="true"
    />
  </package>
</servicing>
```

After adding these Hyper-V components, the creation of our `unattended.xml` file is completed. You can download the complete sample XML file from `http://bit.ly/1xBIQb2`. Place the file in the root folder on the USB drive and boot the Server system from your installation media. You will now experience a fully Zero-Touch Hyper-V installation. In `Chapter 2`, *Deploying Highly Available Hyper-V Clusters*, you will learn how to advance this even further into a Zero-Touch cluster installation.

```
<UILanguage>en-US</UILanguage>
</SetupUILanguage>
<InputLocale>en-US</InputLocale>
<SystemLocale>en-US</SystemLocale>
<UILanguage>en-US</UILanguage>
<UserLocale>en-US</UserLocale>
</component>
- <component language="neutral" xmlns:xsi="http://www.w3.org/2001/XMLSchema-instance"
xmlns:wcm="http://schemas.microsoft.com/WMIConfig/2002/State" versionScope="nonSxS"
publicKeyToken="31bf3856ad364e35" processorArchitecture="x86" name="Microsoft-Windows-
Setup">
    - <DiskConfiguration>
        - <Disk wcm:action="add">
            - <CreatePartitions>
                - <CreatePartition wcm:action="add">
                    <Order>2</Order>
                    <Size>100</Size>
                    <Type>EFI</Type>
                </CreatePartition>
                - <CreatePartition wcm:action="add">
                    <Order>3</Order>
                    <Size>128</Size>
                    <Type>MSR</Type>
                </CreatePartition>
                - <CreatePartition wcm:action="add">
                    <Order>1</Order>
                    <Type>Primary</Type>
                    <Size>350</Size>
                    <Extend>true</Extend>
                </CreatePartition>
            </CreatePartitions>
            - <ModifyPartitions>
                - <ModifyPartition wcm:action="add">
                    <Active>false</Active>
```

Unattended.XML file for automatic Hyper-V setup

The unattended XML file can also be used in **Virtual Machine Manager (VMM)** in the Physical Computer Profiles that enable you to deploy Hyper-V hosts from the VMM console.

Post-installation tasks

Be sure to remove the USB drive with the unattended setup file prior to moving the host to production. A host reboot could otherwise force a reinstallation, including a wipe of all hard drives, due to the trigger of another unattended installation.

Run Windows Update to make sure that you have installed all the available updates. Are there any Windows updates you should not install on Hyper-V hosts? Yes, drivers should not be installed over a Windows Update unless support tells you to do so. However, besides this, install every available Windows Update in all of your Hyper-V hosts.

The Hyper-V role is already enabled, and we are ready to create VMs. To ensure network connectivity and safe operations of our VMs, we will configure some additional parameters after the installation.

First of all, we need some basic network connectivity for our VMs. If you have a second NIC available in your host, run the following command in an elevated PowerShell session:

```
New-VMSwitch -Name SW-1G -NetAdapterName "Local Area Connection 2"
```

If you have only one NIC, run the following command:

```
New-VMSwitch -Name SW-1G-NetAdapterName "Local Area Connection" -
AllowManagementOS $true
```

When the virtual switch is created, you can manage it from Hyper-V manager:

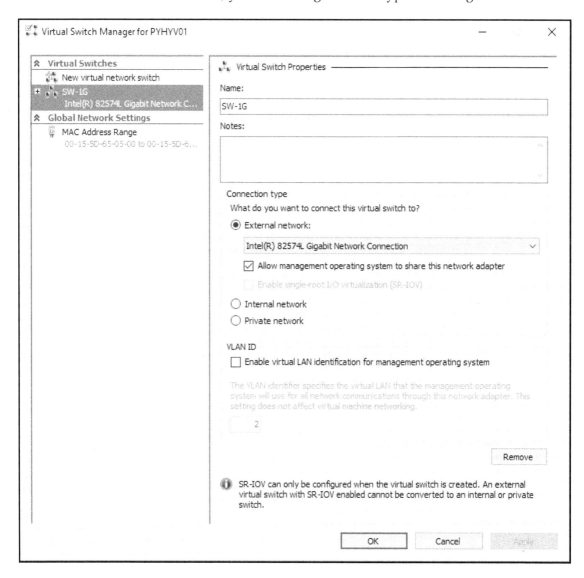

Virtual switch settings from Hyper-V manager

Now, your virtual machines can use an external Hyper-V switch named *external* to communicate over the network.

Ever wondered about the many errors your RDP-mapped printer can create on a Hyper-V host? I could not believe this for a long time, but recently, I have seen a Hyper-V Server with the blue screen due to improper printing drivers. Do you need to print from a Hyper-V host? Absolutely not! So, make sure that you disable RDP Printer Mapping through a Group Policy (or Local Policy).

Navigate to **Computer Configuration** | **Policies** | **Administrative Templates** | **Windows Components** | **Remote Desktop Services** | **Remote Desktop Session Host** | **Printer Redirection** | **Do not allow client printer redirection** and select **Enable** in a Group Policy.

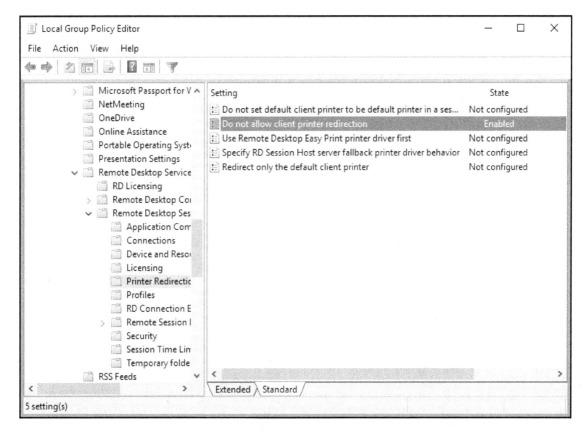

Disable RDP printer mapping

Hyper-V uses some default paths to store virtual machine configuration and its hard disks. I find this very interesting, but it is definitely not suitable for a production environment. Make sure that you change the default paths, if possible to a nonsystem drive, by running the following commands in an elevated PowerShell window:

```
Set-VMHOST -computername localhost -virtualharddiskpath 'D:\VMs'
Set-VMHOST -computername localhost -virtualmachinepath 'D:\VMs'
```

I have not seen any issues in placing VM configuration files and virtual hard disks into the same folder structure. You have everything your VM configuration depends on in one place.

 Another important post-installation task is to follow the rule: **do not install other roles on Hyper-V hosts** except Storage and related features (Hyperconverged model, for example).

A Hyper-V host is a Hyper-V host and nothing else. Move all the other services into virtual machines that run on the Hyper-V host.

Moreover, also keep the following points in mind:

- Do not install any features other than Failover Clustering and **Multipath I/O** (**MPIO**) on a Hyper-V host

   There are exceptions in an SMB3 scenario where you also want to install **Datacenter Bridging** (**DCB**) and SMB bandwidth limits.

- Limit software installations to an absolute minimum, that is, backup and monitoring agents

Antivirus on a Hyper-V host

Another great topic for discussion is whether you should install an antivirus client on a Hyper-V host or not. Many companies have compliance rules stating that on every Server or every Windows machine, an AV client needs to be installed. If there is a rule like this in place, follow it and install an AV agent on your Hyper-V hosts. Make sure that you also implement the long list of files, which contain all the Hyper-V configuration files and virtual machine data, you have to exclude from your scans.

I have seen antivirus engines on Hyper-V hosts doing bad things such as breaking a virtual hard disk, deleting an essential system file, or just producing a very intense amount of storage IOs. Excluding all relevant files and folders regarding Hyper-V and its VMs, there is nothing left worth scanning on a Hyper-V host. If you are not bound by a compliance policy, I highly recommend that you do not install antivirus products on Hyper-V.

There are some approaches for Hyper-V-aware antivirus products; however, I have not seen one flawless working solution as of today, so you should protect your VMs from malware from inside the VM by installing your AV agents into the virtual machines.

Setting the pagefile

One of the most frequent configuration tips around Hyper-V hosts is to manually configure the pagefile. The values described are sometimes quite creative.

After doing many tests with Hyper-V hosts with all different kinds of RAM configurations and deep technology-oriented exchanges with Microsoft Product Teams, including the Hyper-V Product Team itself, on how pagefile management work in Windows Server 2016, there is only one recommendation I have today-leave it alone.

The Windows pagefile is, by default, managed by Windows. If you have followed all other best practices described up to this point, and most importantly, you did not install other services on the Hyper-V host itself (management OS), you are all set. There is no way you can reach the same or even a better efficiency in pagefile management by manually altering this automatic configuration. I have not seen a single Hyper-V installation on Windows Server 2016 as of now that had problems with automatic pagefile management.

Again, this only affects the Hyper-V host and not the pagefile configuration of the virtual machines.

There are some more valuable post-installation tasks for performance management in Chapter 7, *Hyper-V Performance Tuning*. You can manage the pagefile as shown in the following screenshot:

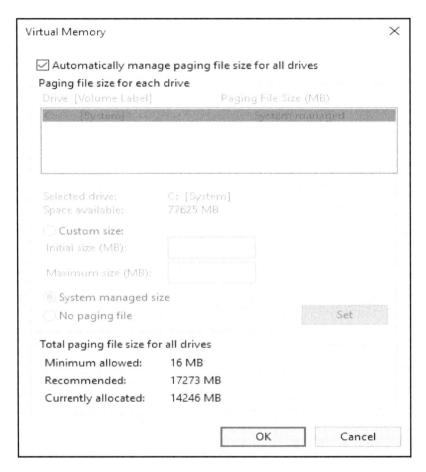

Pagefile configuration

Creating virtual machines

You are all set, and it's time to create some virtual machines. To do a rapid deployment of virtual machines, we will rely on PowerShell.

Creating a new virtual machine with PowerShell is easy; just open an elevated PowerShell prompt, and run the following command:

```
New-VM
```

Without any additional parameters, this will create a new virtual machine with the default parameters. To create a new Generation 2 VM, run the following command:

```
New-VM -Generation 2
```

To create a new virtual machine with a specified name, a custom path to store the VM files, and a memory configuration, run the following command:

```
New-VM -Name VM01 -Path C:\VM01 -Memorystartupbytes 1024MB
```

Your newly created virtual machine doesn't have a hard disk yet. Create a new VHDX file by running the following command:

```
New-VHD -Path C:\vms\vm01\vm01_c.vhdx -SizeBytes 60GB -Dynamic
```

The VHD cmdlet

The created VHDX is not yet attached to a virtual machine. Do this by running the following command:

```
Add-VMHardDiskDrive -VMName VM01 -Path C:\vms\vm01\vm01_c.vhdx
```

To add a network adapter to our virtual machine, run the following command:

```
Add-VMNetworkAdapter -vmname "VM01" -switchname "external"
```

Then, start the VM by running the following command:

```
Start-VM -Name VM01
```

You will recognize that the virtual machine now has all the basic hardware parameters but fails to boot due to a missing operating system. There are multiple ways to create an operating system for a standard VM. The most granular way to achieve this is using Virtual Machine Manager templates (refer to Chapter 8, *Management with System Center and Azure*, for details), but there are great capabilities already included in Windows Server 2016. The approach that is seen most often is to manually install the first virtual machine and include everything you want in each of your virtual machines, such as operating system, updates, and backup agents. Then, sysprep the virtual machine by executing sysprep.exe present at C:\Windows\System32\sysprep\ with the **Generalize** and **OOBE** options and shut down the virtual machine. Copy it to a Template folder and mark this as read only. As of Windows Server 2016, you can even copy and export running virtual machines.

If you need a new virtual machine, just copy the Template folder, rename it with your machine name and a preinstalled operating system with all your previous created configurations are still available.

If you don't like patching all your images and archived VMs manually, you can use a solution to update these VHD/VHDx files offline with Apply-WindowsUpdate.ps1-just another gem from the TechNet Gallery (download this from the shortlink, http://bit.ly/1o4sczI).

As you have seen in this chapter, I have mainly used Generation 2 VMs. If your guest operating systems are Windows Server 2012 and higher, this should be your default option. Generation 2 VMs allow faster booting, better stability, and smaller attack surface through a greatly reduced set of legacy hardware.

Summary

With the tools from this chapter and the configuration files you have already created up to now, you will be able to deploy new Hyper-V hosts and VMs faster and in a more reliable way than ever before. Besides this, you learned valuable best practices to plan and configure your single Hyper-V host.

In Chapter 2, *Deploying Highly Available Hyper-v Clusters*, you will learn to create high-availability solutions based on your current setup to leverage additional capabilities of Hyper-V and virtualization.

2
Deploying Highly Available Hyper-V Clusters

"Live Migration between hosts in a Hyper-V cluster is very straightforward and requires no specific configuration, apart from type and amount of simultaneous Live Migrations. If you add multiple clusters and standalone Hyper-V hosts into the mix, I strongly advise you to configure Kerberos Constrained Delegation for all hosts and clusters involved."

Hans Vredevoort – MVP Hyper-V

This chapter will guide you through the installation of Hyper-V clusters and their best-practice configuration. After installing the first Hyper-V host, it may be necessary to add another layer of availability to your virtualization services. With Failover Clusters, you get independence from hardware failures and are protected from planned or unplanned service outages.

This chapter includes the following topics:

- Prerequirements and implementation of Failover Clusters
- Cluster and quorum configuration
- Live Migration and Live Migration protocols
- Guest clustering and shared hard disk files
- VM start ordering

Preparing for a high availability scenario

As with every project, **high availability (HA)** scenario starts with a planning phase. Virtualization projects often turn up the question of additional availability for the first time in an environment. In traditional datacenters with physical server systems and local storage systems, an outage of a hardware component will affect only one server hosting one service. The source of the outage can be localized very fast and the affected parts can be replaced in a short time. Server virtualization comes with great benefits, such as improved operating efficiency and reduced hardware dependencies. However, a single component failure can impact a lot of virtualized systems at once. By adding redundant systems, these single points of failure can be avoided.

Planning an HA environment

The most important factor in whether you need a HA environment is your business requirements. You need to find out how often and how long an IT-related production service can be interrupted, unplanned, or planned, without causing a serious problem to your business. Those requirements are defined in a central IT strategy of a business as well as in process definitions that are IT-driven. They include service-level agreements of critical business services run in the various departments of your company. If those definitions do not exist or are unavailable, talk to the process owners to determine the level of availability needed. HA is structured in different classes and measured by the total uptime in a defined timespan, which is 99.999 percent in a year. Every nine in this figure adds a huge amount of complexity and money needed to ensure this availability, so take the time to find out the real availability needed by your services and resist the temptation to plan running every service on multiredundant, geo-spread cluster systems, as it may not fit the budget.

Be sure to plan for additional capacity in an HA environment, so that you can lose hardware components without the need to sacrifice application performance.

Overview of the failover cluster

A Hyper-V Failover Cluster consists of two or more Hyper-V Server compute nodes. Technically, it's possible to use a Failover Cluster with just one computing node; however, it will not provide any availability advantages over a standalone host and is typically only used for migration scenarios.

I don't recommend you to implement a Hyper-V cluster in production without at least three nodes. A single node cluster doesn't ensure high availability. A two-node cluster is not efficient because half of the resources are dedicated to high availability.

A Failover Cluster hosts roles such as Hyper-V virtual machines on its computing nodes. If one node fails due to a hardware problem, it will no longer perform cluster heartbeat communication, even though the service interruption is almost instantly detected. The virtual machines running on that particular node are powered off immediately because of the hardware failure on their computing node. The remaining cluster nodes then immediately take over these VMs in an unplanned failover process and start them on their own respective hardware. The virtual machines will be a backup, running after a successful boot of their operating systems and applications in just a few minutes. Hyper-V Failover Clusters work on the condition that all compute nodes have access to a shared storage instance, holding the virtual machine configuration data and its virtual hard disks. In the case of a planned failover, that is, for patching compute nodes, it's possible to move running virtual machines from one cluster node to another without interrupting the VM. All cluster nodes can run virtual machines at the same time, as long as there is enough failover capacity running all services when a node goes down. Even though a Hyper-V cluster is still called a Failover Cluster, utilizing the Windows Server Failover Clustering feature, it is indeed capable of running an Active/Active Cluster.

To ensure that all these capabilities of a Failover Cluster are indeed working demands an accurate planning and implementation process.

Failover cluster prerequirements

To successfully implement a Hyper-V Failover Cluster, we need suitable hardware, software, permissions, and network and storage infrastructure as outlined in the following sections.

Hardware requirements

The hardware used in a Failover Cluster environment needs to be validated against the Windows Server Catalog, as we did in `Chapter 1`, *Accelerating Hyper-V Deployment*. Microsoft will only support Hyper-V clusters when all components are certified for Windows Server 2016.

The servers used to run our HA virtual machines should ideally consist of identical hardware models with identical components. It is possible, and supported, to run servers in the same cluster with different hardware components, that is, with different sizes of RAM; however, due to a higher level of complexity, this is not the best practice.

Special planning considerations are needed to address the CPU requirements of a cluster. To ensure maximum compatibility, all CPUs in a cluster should be exactly the same model. While it's possible, from a technical point of view, to mix even CPUs from Intel and AMD in the same cluster though to a different architecture, you will lose core cluster capabilities such as **live migration**.

Choosing a single vendor for your CPUs is not enough. Even when using different CPU models, your cluster nodes may be using a different set of CPU instruction set extensions. With different instructions sets, live migrations won't work either. There is a compatibility mode that disables most of the instruction set on all CPUs on all cluster nodes; however, this leaves you with a negative impact on performance and should be avoided. A better approach to this problem would be to create another cluster from the legacy CPUs running smaller or nonproduction workloads without affecting your high-performance production workloads.

If you want to extend your cluster after some time, you will find yourself with the problem of not having exactly the same hardware available for purchase. Choose the current revision of the model or product line you are already using in your cluster and manually compare the CPU instruction sets at `http://ark.intel.com/` and `http://products.amd.com/`. Choose the current CPU model that best fits the original CPU features of your cluster, and have this design validated by your hardware partner.

Ensure that your servers are equipped with compatible CPUs, the same amount of RAM, and the same network cards and storage controllers.

Network design

Mixing different vendors of network cards in a single server is fine and the best practice for availability, but make sure that all your Hyper-V hosts are using an identical hardware setup. A network adapter should only be used exclusively for LAN traffic or storage traffic. Do not mix these two types of communication in any basic scenario. There are some more advanced scenarios involving converged networking that can enable mixed traffic, but in most cases, this is a not good idea. A Hyper-V Failover Cluster requires multiple layers of communication between its nodes and storage systems. Hyper-V networking and storage options have changed dramatically through the different releases of Hyper-V. With Windows Server 2016, network design options are endless; refer to Chapter 5, *Network Best Practices*, for details. In this chapter, we will work with a typically seen basic set of network designs. We have at least six NICs available in our servers with a bandwidth of 1 GB/s. If you have more than five interface cards available per server, use Switch Embedded Teaming to ensure the availability of the network or even use converged networking (both features are also introduced in Chapter 5, *Network Best Practices*). Converged networking will also be your choice if you have fewer than five network adapters available. To ease the explanation, let's think about a host with the following six network adapters:

1. The first NIC will be exclusively used for host communication with our Hyper-V host and will not be involved in the VM network traffic or cluster communication at any time. It will ensure Active Directory and management traffic to our Management OS.
2. The second NIC will ensure live migration of virtual machines between our cluster nodes.
3. The third NIC will be used for VM traffic. Our virtual machines will be connected to the various production and lab networks through this NIC.
4. The fourth NIC will be used for internal cluster communication. The first four NICs can either be teamed through Windows Server or can be abstracted from the physical hardware through Windows Server network virtualization and converged fabric design using Switch Embedded Teaming.
5. The fifth NIC will be reserved for storage communication. As advised, we will be isolating storage and production LAN communication from each other. If you do not use iSCSI storage communication, this NIC will not be necessary. If you use Fibre Channel SAN technology, use a FC-HBA instead. If you leverage **Direct Attached Storage** (**DAS**), use the appropriate connector for storage communication.

6. The sixth NIC will also be used for storage communication as a redundancy. The redundancy will be established via MPIO and not via NIC Teaming except for SMB3-based storage and the hyperconverged model where we will use SMB Multichannel.

There is no need for a dedicated heartbeat network as in the older revisions of Windows Server with Hyper-V. All cluster networks will automatically be used for sending heartbeat signals throughout the other cluster members.

If you don't have 1 GB/s interfaces available, or if you use 10 GbE adapters, the best practice is to implement the converged networking solution described in `Chapter 5`, *Network Best Practices*.

In many environments, you will have several physical adapters or virtual adapters. For better manageability, I recommend you to rename the network adapters. In projects where I am involved, I always rename them with their purposes and the VLAN numbers. The following is an example:

- Management NIC (VLAN ID 10): This was renamed as **Management-10**
- Live-Migration NIC (VLAN ID 11): This was renamed as **LiveMigration-11**
- Heartbeat NIC (VLAN ID 12): This was renamed as **Heartbeat-12**

With this naming convention, I can identify quickly the network interface and the VLAN ID.

Storage design

All cluster nodes must have access to the virtual machines residing on a centrally shared storage medium. This could be a classic setup with a SAN, a NAS, or a more modern concept with Windows Scale-Out File Servers hosting virtual machine files, SMB3 file shares, or a hyperconverged model. Refer to `Chapter 4`, *Storage Best Practices*, for more information on finding the right storage solution for you. In this chapter, we will use a NetApp SAN system capable of providing a classic SAN approach with LUNs mapped to our hosts as well as utilizing SMB3 file shares, but any other Windows Server 2016 validated SAN will also fulfill the requirements.

In our first setup, we will utilize **Cluster Shared Volumes** (**CSVs**) to store several virtual machines on the same storage volume. It's not good these days to create a single volume per virtual machine due to the massive management overhead. It's a good rule of thumb to create one CSV per cluster node; in larger environments with more than eight hosts, a CSV per two to four cluster nodes is required. To utilize CSVs, follow these steps:

1. Ensure that all components (SAN, Firmware, HBAs, and so on) are validated for Windows Server 2016 and are up-to-date.
2. Connect your SAN physically to all your Hyper-V hosts via iSCSI or Fibre Channel connections.
3. Create two LUNs on your SAN for hosting virtual machines. Activate Hyper-V performance options for these LUNs if possible (that is, on a NetApp, by setting the LUN type to Hyper-V). Size the LUNs for enough capacity to host all your virtual hard disks.
4. Label the LUNs, CSV01, and CSV02 with appropriate LUN IDs.
5. Create another small LUN of 1 GB and label it `Quorum`.
6. Make the LUNs available to all Hyper-V hosts in this specified cluster by mapping it on the storage device.
7. Do not make these LUNs available to any other hosts or cluster.
8. Prepare storage DSMs and drivers (that is, MPIO) for Hyper-V host installation.
9. Refresh the disk configuration on hosts, install drivers and DSMs, and format volumes as NTFS (quick).
10. Install Microsoft Multipath IO when using redundant storage paths:

```
Install-WindowsFeature -Name Multipath-IO
-Computername Pyhyv01, Pyhyv02
```

In this example, I added the MPIO feature to two Hyper-V hosts with the computer names `Pyhyv01` and `Pyhyv02`.

SANs are typically equipped with two storage controllers for redundancy reasons. Make sure to disperse your workloads over both controllers for optimal availability and performance.

Once the LUN is available in the Hyper-V host, I recommend you to rename the volume and the CSV (in failover clustering manager) with the same name that you have provided in the storage device. This configuration eases the identification of the storage from the Hyper-V hosts and storage device perspective.

If you leverage file servers providing SMB3 shares, the preceding steps do not apply to you. Perform the following steps instead:

1. Create a storage space with the desired disk types and use storage tiering if possible.
2. Create a new SMB3 file share for applications.
3. Customize Permissions to include all Hyper-V servers from the planned clusters as well as the Hyper-V cluster object itself with full control.

For more details on storage design and configuration, refer to Chapter 4, *Storage Best Practices*.

Server and software requirements

In Chapter 1, *Accelerating Hyper-V Deployment*, you installed your first Hyper-V host. To create a Failover Cluster, you need to install a second Hyper-V host. Use the same unattended file but change the IP address and the hostname. Join both Hyper-V hosts to your Active Directory domain if you have not done this yet. Hyper-V can be clustered without leveraging Active Directory, but lacks several key components, such as live migration, and shouldn't be done on purpose. The availability to successfully boot up a domain-joined Hyper-V cluster without the need to have an Active Directory domain controller present during boot time is the major benefit from the Active Directory independency of Failover Clusters.

Ensure that you create a Hyper-V virtual switch as shown earlier with the same name on both hosts to ensure cluster compatibility, and that both nodes are installed with all updates.

If you have System Center 2016 in place, use the System Center Virtual Machine Manager to create a Hyper-V cluster (refer to Chapter 8, *Management with System Center and Azure*); otherwise, continue with this chapter.

Implementing failover clusters

Having prepared our Hyper-V hosts, we will now create a Failover Cluster using PowerShell. I'm assuming that your hosts are installed, the storage and network connections are prepared, and the Hyper-V role is already active utilizing up-to-date drivers and firmware on your hardware:

1. First, we need to ensure that the server name, date, and time of our hosts are correct. Time and time zone configurations should occur via Group Policy.

2. For automatic network configuration later on, it's important to rename the network connections from the defaults to their designated roles using PowerShell, as shown in the following commands:

```
Rename-NetAdapter -Name "Ethernet" -NewName "Host"
Rename-NetAdapter -Name "Ethernet 2" -NewName
"LiveMig"
Rename-NetAdapter -Name "Ethernet 3" -NewName "VMs"
Rename-NetAdapter -Name "Ethernet 4" -NewName
"Cluster"
Rename-NetAdapter -Name "Ethernet 5" -NewName
"Storage"
```

The **Network Connections** window should look like the following screenshot:

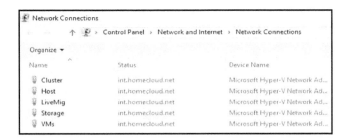

Hyper-V host Network Connections

3. Next, we need to set the IP configuration of the network adapters. If you are not using DHCP for your servers, manually set the IP configuration (different subnets) of the specified network cards. A great blog post on how to automate this step is available at `http://bit.ly/Upa5bJ`.

4. Next, we need to activate the necessary Failover Clustering features on both of our Hyper-V hosts:

```
Install-WindowsFeature -Name Failover-Clustering
-IncludeManagementTools `
-Computername pyhyv01, pyhyv02
```

5. Before actually creating the cluster, we will launch a cluster validation cmdlet via PowerShell:

```
Test-Cluster pyhyv01, pyhyv02
```

Open the generated `.mht` file for more details, as shown in the following screenshot:

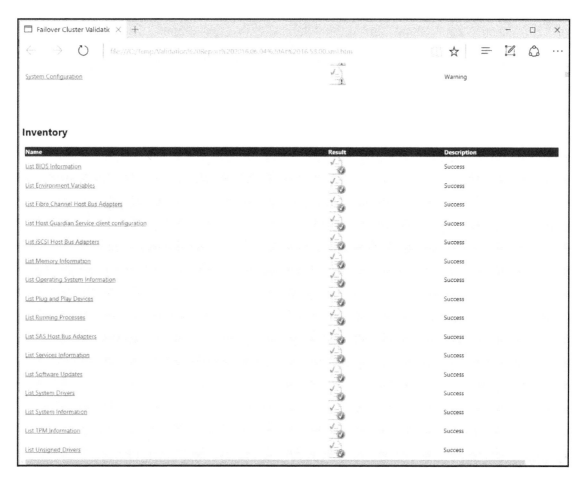

Cluster validation

As you can see, there are some warnings that should be investigated. However, as long as there are no errors, the configuration is ready for clustering and fully supported by Microsoft. However, check out **Warning** to ensure that you won't run into problems in the long run. After you have fixed potential errors and warnings listed in the Cluster Validation Report, you can finally create the cluster as follows:

```
New-Cluster
-Name CN=Cluster-Hyv01,OU=Servers,DC=int,DC=homecloud,DC=Net
-Node Pyhyv01, Pyhyv02 `
-StaticAddress 192.168.1.49
```

This will create a new cluster named `Cluster-Hyv01`, consisting of the nodes `Pyhyv01` and `Pyhyv02` and using the cluster IP address `192.168.1.49`.

This cmdlet will create the cluster and the corresponding Active Directory object in the specified OU. Moving the cluster object to a different OU later on will not be a problem at all; even renaming it is possible when done the right way.

After creating the cluster, when you open the **Failover Cluster Manager** console, you should be able to connect to your cluster, as shown here:

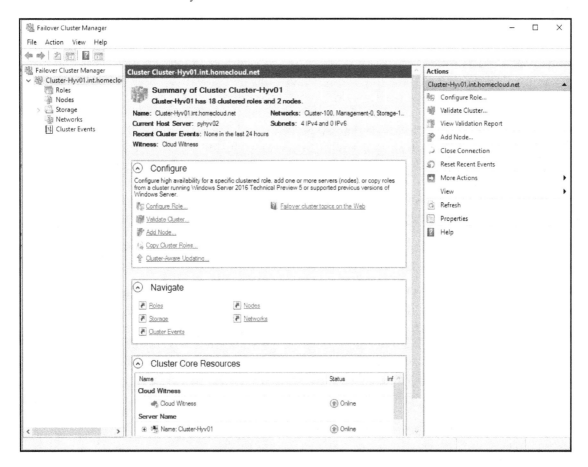

Failover Cluster Manager

You will see that all your cluster nodes and **Cluster Core Resources** are online. Rerun the Validation Report and copy the generated .htm files to a secure location if you need them for support queries. Keep in mind that you have to rerun this wizard if any hardware or configuration changes occur in the cluster components, including any of its nodes.

The initial cluster setup is now complete and we can continue with the post-creation tasks.

Quorum configuration

The quorum is a very important part of a cluster. The quorum helps to maintain the data integrity and avoids split-brain situations. If the network connections between the cluster nodes fail, a cluster node in an even-node setup would have no information if it is part of the isolated area through the outage and has to shut down all cluster services. If it is in the remaining part of the network, it would have to take over cluster services being offline due to the outage. For a successful vote determining which node or nodes are to take over the production service, a total of more than 50 percent of all cluster nodes will need to communicate. If, like in our situation with a two-node cluster, not more than 50 percent of the nodes are available, the node shuts down all its cluster services. In our scenario, both nodes stop all services and our cluster is completely offline to protect us from a split-brain situation. A quorum is another instance of getting to vote and ensuring that a majority of cluster resources are available to do a successful vote. In our configuration, the smallest storage volume got assigned as a quorum automatically. That's why we created a 1 GB LUN earlier. Using this LUN as a quorum ensures that there is a majority of votes available in an event that partitions an even-node cluster, such as a network outage.

In Windows Server 2012, Microsoft brought in Dynamic quorum, which enables assigning votes to a node dynamically to avoid losing the majority of votes and so that the cluster can run with one node (known as the **last-man standing**). Dynamic quorum works great when the failures are sequential and not simultaneous. So, for a stretched cluster scenario, if you lose a room, the failure is simultaneous and the dynamic quorum does not have the time to recalculate the majority of votes; this is why the witness should be placed in a third room.

The dynamic quorum has been enhanced in Windows Server 2012 R2. Now, the dynamic witness is implemented. This feature calculates whether the quorum witness has a vote. There are two cases, which are as follows:

- If there is an even number of nodes in the cluster with the dynamic quorum enabled, the dynamic witness is enabled on the quorum witness and so the witness has a vote

- If there is an odd number of nodes in the cluster with the dynamic quorum enabled, the dynamic witness is enabled on the quorum witness and so the witness does not have a vote

So, since Windows Server 2012 R2, Microsoft recommends you always implement a witness in a cluster and let the dynamic quorum decide for you. The dynamic quorum has been enabled by default since Windows Server 2012.

A witness can either be a logical disk, a file share, or, since Windows Server 2016, a cloud witness. There are several reasons why you should prefer a disk witness over a file share witness if possible; for instance, the disk-based witness will host a complete copy of the cluster database whereas the file share witness won't. The cloud witness can also be a good option in the case of a stretched cluster between two rooms. A cloud witness brings you an external location for the witness at a low cost.

With the recent version of Hyper-V, you won't have to think about when to choose a quorum and how to configure it. You just specify a disk witness, if available, or a file share; otherwise, Failover Clustering automatically configures the necessary settings, regardless of the number of nodes. If you are currently using a two-node cluster and plan to add more cluster nodes later, you won't have to change the quorum model later. There are options to change the vote counts of the various resources, and the best practice is not to change them in typical cluster configurations. Quorum changes can occur online, and we can achieve this through PowerShell:

```
Set-ClusterQuorum -NodeAndDiskMajority "Cluster Disk
2"
```

The preceding line represents `Cluster Disk 2` as the label of the cluster resource. If you are using a file share witness, use the following option:

```
Set-ClusterQuorum -NodeAndFileShareMajority
\\File01\Share01
```

To finish, if you want to use a cloud witness, use the following PowerShell cmdlet:

```
Set-ClusterQuorum -CloudWitness
-AccountName StorageAccountName>
-AccessKey <AccessKey>
```

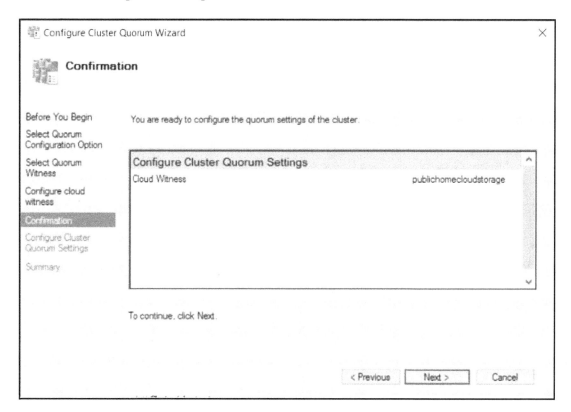

Cluster Quorum Wizard

Live migration configuration

Live migration describes the ability to move running virtual machines between Hyper-V hosts. Since Windows Server 2012, this capability is not an exclusive cluster feature anymore, but most of the time they are utilized inside a cluster. You can use live migrations between standalone hosts or between different clusters as well; a shared-nothing live migration will occur, moving not just the RAM of the virtual machine but all of its virtual hard disks, which may consume a lot of network bandwidth and time. Typically, shared-nothing live migrations are used in migration processes and not in day-to-day work.

A live migration of virtual machines occurs every time a planned failover is executed on a Hyper-V cluster. The RAM of the virtual machine is synchronized between the nodes; the handles for the virtual machine configuration and its virtual hard disks are then failed-over to the new host. It's one of the most widely used features in Hyper-V, but often configured incorrectly.

An important aspect of the live migration process is the machine-based authentication. CredSSP is the default authentication protocol in Windows Server 2016. It is easy to use, but it's not the most secure solution and not recommended for production systems. If only one system gets compromised in the chain of delegation, all systems used in the CredSSP environment are compromised as well. Besides that, if you are using CredSSP for live migrations, you will have to log on to the source host first to initiate the migration process due to the one-hop limitation of CredSSP.

If your Hyper-V hosts are part of the same Active Directory domain—and in most cases they will be—you can use the Kerberos protocol for live migration authentication, which offers more security and gets around the limitations of CredSSP. Furthermore, it lets you define granular limits where the account credentials can be used. Use PowerShell to set constraint delegations on a system with Active Directory Management tools installed for all Hyper-V hosts involved, with the following script:

```
$Host = "pyhyv01"
$Domain = "int.homecloud.net"
Get-ADComputer pyhyv01 | Set-ADObject -Add @{"msDS-
AllowedToDelegateTo"="Microsoft Virtual System Migration
Service/$Host.$Domain", "cifs/$Host.$Domain","Microsoft Virtual System
Migration Service/$Host", "cifs/$Host"}
```

Be sure to reboot the hosts afterwards so that this configuration can become active.

However, this will just allow `pyhyv01` to delegate its credentials to `pyhyv02`. You have to do this vice versa on your two-node cluster. For bigger clusters, there is a script that enables all combinations for all your Hyper-V hosts (put them in a single OU, the best practice for many reasons) at `http://bit.ly/1hC0S9W`.

After we have prepared our Active Directory for Kerberos constraint delegation, we will activate incoming and outgoing live migrations for our Hyper-V hosts:

```
Enable-VMMigration -Computername pyhyv01, pyhyv02
Set-VMHost -Computername pyhyv01, pyhyv02
    -VirtualMachineMigrationAuthenticationType Kerberos
```

Live migrations are enabled using compression by default. RAM will be compressed to a ZIP-like archive before transmission and extracted on the target host. This is a great setting if you are using 1 GB/s NICs for live migration as it uses spare CPU cycles to compress live migrations to speed up the transfer. If you are using 10 GB/s network connections, switch live migrations to SMB3 for even better performance. Also, we increase the limit for continuous live migrations from two (great for 1 GB/s) to four simultaneous live migrations:

```
Set-VMHost -Computername pyhyv01, pyhyv02
    -MaximumVirtualMachineMigrations 4
    -MaximumStorageMigrations 4
    -VirtualMachineMigrationPerformanceOption SMBTransport
```

You can also configure these settings through the GUI of every cluster node, as shown here:

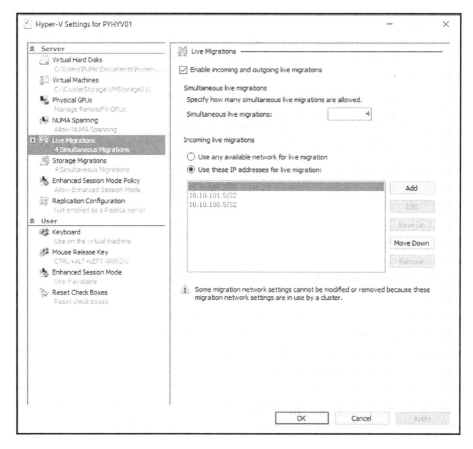

Live Migration options

Use the following command and later switch back to the defaults, if needed:

```
Set-VMHost -Computername pyhyv01, pyhyv02
-MaximumVirtualMachineMigrations 2
-MaximumStorageMigrations 2
-VirtualMachineMigrationPerformanceOption Compression
```

In the GUI, the preceding command will reflect the changes, as shown here:

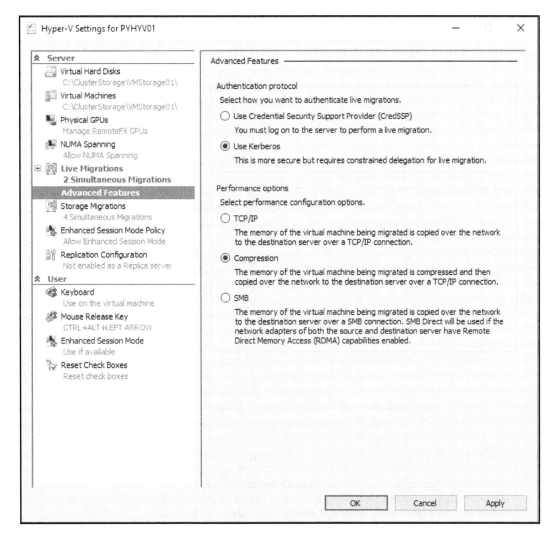

Advanced live migration options

The last setting for preparing live migrations is to choose the network for live migration. By default, all available networks are enabled for live migration. We don't change that. If our live migration network is unavailable and we quickly need to free up a host, we will use other available networks as well; however, by specifying a lower priority (the default is greater than 5.000) to our live migration network, we ensure it is preferred for live migrations:

```
Set-VMMigrationNework 192.168.10.* -Priority 4.000
(Get-ClusterNetwork -Name "Live-Migration").Role = 1
```

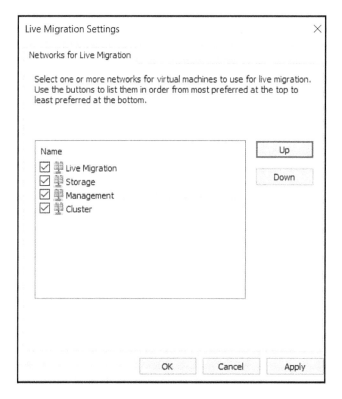

Live migration settings

We also set the basic configuration for the other cluster networks, as follows:

```
(Get-ClusterNetwork -Name "Management ").Role = 3
Set-VMMigrationNework 192.168.10.* -Priority 4.000
(Get-ClusterNetwork -Name "Cluster").Role = 1
(Get-ClusterNetwork -Name "Cluster").Metric = 3.000
(Get-ClusterNetwork -Name "Storage").Role = 0
```

The final network configuration should now look like the following screenshot:

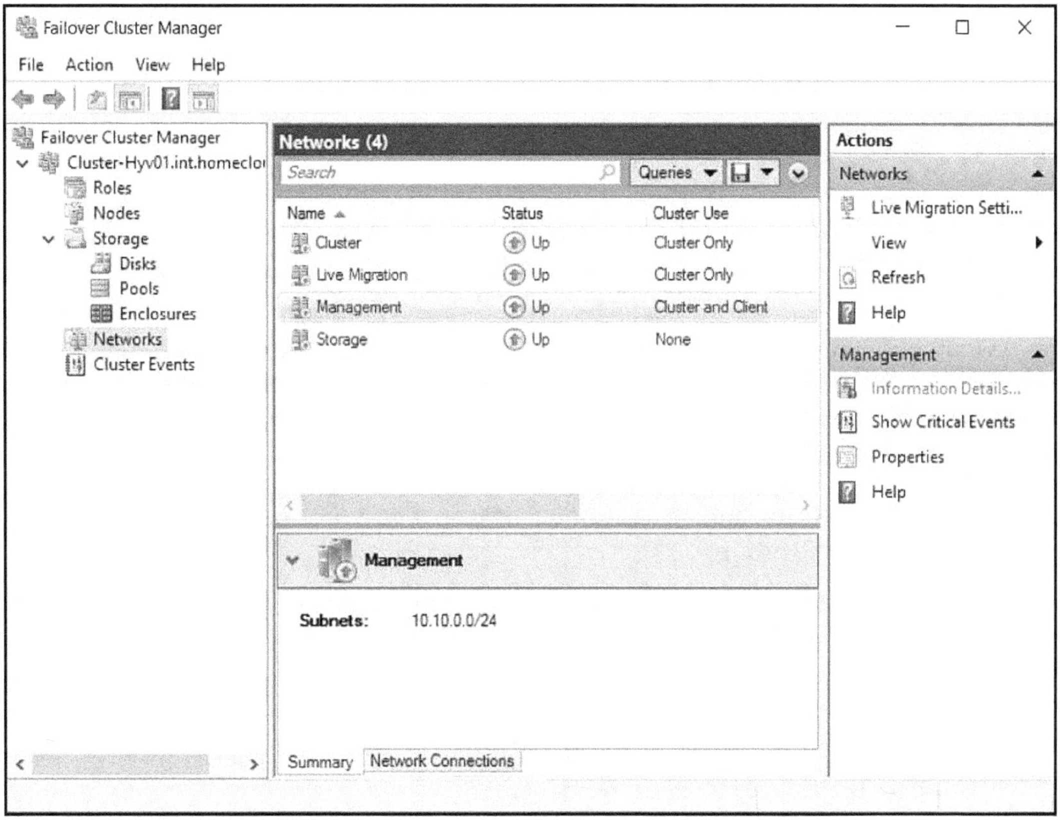

Cluster network configuration

After that configuration, we are ready to initiate our first live migration. To do this, simply execute the following on our first host:

```
Move-VM "VM01" Pyhyv02
```

If you want to live migrate all virtual machines from one host to another, use the following cmdlet:

```
Suspend-ClusterNode -Name Pyhyv01 -Target Pyhyv02 -
Drain
```

We are now finished with the configuration of our host cluster. For more advanced monitoring and tuning configurations for Failover Clusters, refer to Chapter 7, *Hyper-V Performance Tuning*.

You are now ready to test your cluster configuration before putting it into production. Power off a running cluster node hosting virtual machines by removing the power cables and see what's happening to your cluster. Do not use the `Shutdown` command or the buttons on the server as this would not be a real-life test.

VM start ordering

Prior to Windows Server 2016, it was not easy to start a VM in the chosen order because it was based on priority (low, medium, and high) and/or an automatic startup delay in second.

Since Windows Server 2016, we can start a VM or a group of VMs in the chosen order by implementing dependencies between them. A group can hold a single VM or multiple VMs. This is why I recommend you always create a group even if a single VM belongs to a group. If later you want to add a VM to a step that does not involve a group in the VM start ordering plan, you have to remove the dependencies, create a group, add the VMs to the group, and again create dependencies. Instead, if you have created only groups, you just have to add the VM to a group.

The following example will create three groups called `SQLServers`, `VMMServers`, and `OMGServers`. The `VMMServers` and `OMGServers` groups will be dependent on the `SQLServers` group. To create the groups, just run the following PowerShell cmdlet:

```
New-ClusterGroupSet -Name SQLServers
New-ClusterGroupSet -Name VMMServers
New-ClusterGroupSet -Name OMGServers
```

The following PowerShell cmdlet configure the groups to be ready when the group has reached an online state. This means that the VMs in the dependent group will not start until the dependent group is online:

```
Set-ClusterGroupSet -Name SQLServers -StartupSetting Online
Set-ClusterGroupSet -Name VMMServers -StartupSetting Online
Set-ClusterGroupSet -Name OMGServers -StartupSetting Online
```

Now, create the dependencies between `SQLServers` and `VMMServers`, then between `SQLServers` and `OMGServers`:

```
Add-ClusterGroupSetDependency -Name VMMServers -
ProviderSet SQLServers
Add-ClusterGroupSetDependency -Name OMGServers -
ProviderSet SQLServers
```

Finally, add the related VMs to the groups:

```
Add-ClusterGroupToSet -Name VMVMM01 -Group VMMServers
Add-ClusterGroupToSet -Name VMVMM02 -Group VMMServers
Add-ClusterGroupToSet -Name VMSQL01 -Group SQLServers
Add-ClusterGroupToSet -Name VMSQL02 -Group SQLServers
Add-ClusterGroupToSet -Name VMOMG01 -Group OMGServers
```

Node fairness

Node fairness is an enhancement of the Failover Clustering feature in Windows Server 2016. It enables balancing virtual machines across the cluster node. It is enabled by default. If you manage your cluster from System Center Virtual Machine Manager, this feature is disabled for the benefit of dynamic optimization:

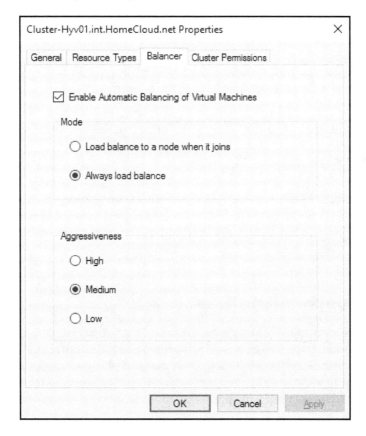

Node fairness configuration

You can configure the aggressiveness and the behavior of the automatic balancing using PowerShell. Before using cmdlet to configure these settings, it is important to understand each value. For aggressiveness, you can refer to the following table:

AutoBalancerLevel	Aggressiveness	Host load percentage
1 (the default)	Low	80%
2	Medium	70%
3	High	60%

For the automatic balancer behavior, you can refer to these values:

AutoBalancerMode	Behavior
0	Disabled
1	Balance on node join only
2 (the default)	Balance on node join and every 30 minutes

To change the default value of these settings, you can run the following PowerShell cmdlet:

```
(Get-Cluster).AutoBalancerLevel = 3
(Get-Cluster).AutoBalancerMode = 1
```

There are no best practices for these settings. It depends on your application and whether you want the system to manage VM balancing. However, I recommend you to avoid being too aggressive because every 30 minutes the system can choose to migrate the VM.

Cluster-Aware Updating

Since you can move running workloads between cluster nodes without affecting production application performance, we will now add **Cluster-Aware Updating** (**CAU**), allowing our Hyper-V cluster to install updates by itself. This is a must-have configuration to ensure low maintenance operations for your Hyper-V clusters. CAU will automatically download and install updates to all cluster nodes utilizing live migrations.

In this way, we can update our cluster any time of the day without the need for service downtime. Execute the following cmdlet on one of the cluster nodes:

```
Add-CauClusterRole -ClusterName Cluster-Hyv01 -Force -
CauPluginName
Microsoft.WindowsUpdatePlugin -MaxRetriesPerNode 3 -
CauPluginArguments @{
'IncludeRecommendedUpdates' = 'True' } -StartDate
"5/6/2014 3:00:00 AM" -
DaysOfWeek 4 -WeeksOfMonth @(3) -verbose
```

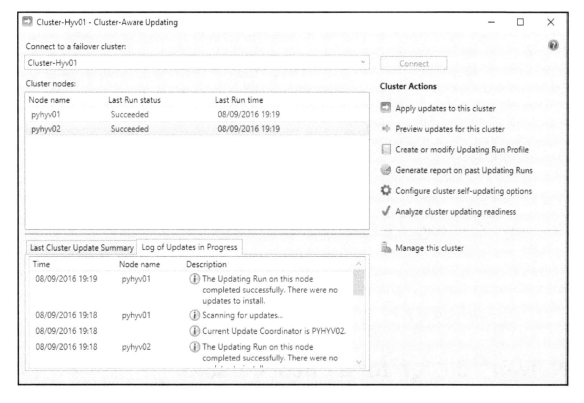

Cluster-Aware Updating Console

You can even utilize an existing WSUS-Server as updating clusters has never been easier. Additional guidance is available for CAU in the Altaro blog at http://bit.ly/V17y24.

Guest clustering

After creating a Hyper-V Failover Cluster on the host level, it is now time to create a guest cluster. A guest cluster is also a Failover Cluster and works the same way as our host cluster; however, its hosting applications are on top of operating systems instead of virtual machine workloads. A guest cluster is used in conjunction with a host cluster to ensure an even higher availability. Do not create guest clusters unless you are already using a host cluster; it won't increase availability to your services in a hardware failure scenario. However, they are great for planned failovers for maintenance purposes on one node.

The basic concepts and cluster creation are identical to the host cluster, that is running, the Cluster Validation Wizard successfully in order to receive support. However, with two running VMs hosting the same service, that is, a production ERP application, you should avoid running these two VMs on the same physical node on your Hyper-V cluster. You can achieve this using anti-affinity rules that ensure the VMs are placed on different hosts. This is possible via System Center Virtual Machine Manager (refer to `Chapter 7`, *Hyper-V Performance Tuning*) or with PowerShell. It is not possible with Failover Cluster Manager GUI. We will continue with the PowerShell approach for now. To create a new anti-affinity rule, execute the following commands:

```
(Get-ClusterGroup ERP-VM1).AntiAffinityClassNames =
"GuestClusterERP1"
(Get-ClusterGroup ERP-VM2).AntiAffinityClassNames =
"GuestClusterERP1"
```

These VMs won't be placed on the same host if possible. Check your current anti-affinity rules affecting a virtual machine by executing the following command:

```
Get-ClusterGroup VM1 | fl anti*
```

Network design for a guest cluster

Since we are already operating in a virtual world, our network setup for our guest cluster is simplified. We just need the following three types of networks instead of five:

- **Client network**: This is used for client connections to our applications and should be configured with `Role = 0`
- **Cluster network**: This serves the same purpose as that on the host cluster; configure it with the equivalent values
- **Storage network**: This serves the same purpose as that on the host cluster; configure it with the equivalent values

These networks need to be configured on the guest cluster additionally to any host cluster networks.

The best practice in a guest-cluster environment is to change the default failover-triggering heartbeat times to allow the execution of live migrations without any cluster activities. To change this from 10 seconds (the default value and suitable for physical clusters) to 25 seconds (TCP time-outs for live migrations are typically up to 20 seconds), execute the following PowerShell cmdlet:

```
(Get-Cluster).CrossSubnetThreshold = 25
(Get-Cluster).SameSubnetThreshold = 25
```

Storage design for a guest cluster

While our network setup benefits from the virtual world, the storage design is more complicated through an added layer of complexity. Just like our host cluster, the guest cluster needs shared storage between the two virtual machines, leaving us with the following storage options:

- **Shared VHDX**: This new feature of Windows Server 2012 R2 allows multiple VMs to connect to a single virtual hard disk if it's prepared accordingly.
- **VHD Set**: This is a new virtual hard disk format of Windows Server 2016 and it is not supported for operating systems earlier than Windows Server 2016. This format is for shared virtual hard disks only. The file format is VHDS.
- **Virtual Fibre Channel**: This new feature of Windows Server 2012 allows us to pass through a Fibre Channel SAN LUN to virtual machines if you are using FC storage.
- **iSCSI**: Connect to a iSCSI target with the iSCSI Initiator from within the VM if you are using iSCSI storage.

The last two storage options are explained further in Chapter 4, *Storage Best Practices*. We will use a VHD Set file to create our Failover Cluster:

1. Create two virtual machines with the Failover Clustering feature enabled and place them on your cluster shared volumes.

2. Create two new VHDS, one as the quorum and the other for data:

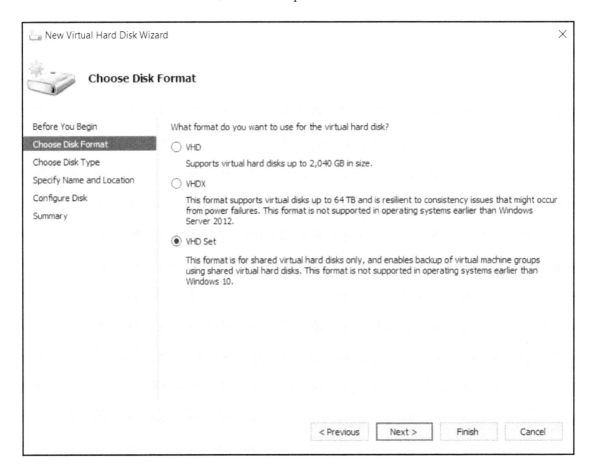

Creating VHD Set

3. Once the VHD Set is created, you can add a new shared drive bound to the SCSI Controller. It is necessary to repeat this task for each VM that shares the VHD Set.

4. Create the guest cluster using the VHDS files as central storage. Install your application to host all data on the shared storage.

You should choose a VHDS when using SMB3 storage since you are not connecting any LUNs to your Hyper-V clusters directly.

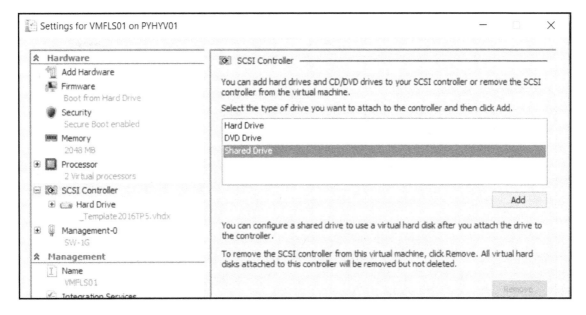

Adding a shared drive to VM

Summary

With the knowledge from this chapter, you are now able to design and implement Hyper-V Failover Clusters as well as guest clusters. You are aware of the basic concepts of HA and the storage and networking options necessary to achieve this. You have seen real-world proven configurations to ensure a stable operating environment.

Now progress to `Chapter 3`, *Backup and Disaster Recovery*, to ensure that your services still run even if a disaster occurs, and be prepared to recover your data!

3
Backup and Disaster Recovery

Whether you are using Windows Server Backup, Azure Backup, Azure Site Recovery, Hyper-V Replica, or any third-party data protection solution, you need to clearly define your RTO and RPO goals and adapt your strategy with a new technology that understands your virtualization platform. The days of a single solution fits all are also over, only a layered approach with different technologies will give you the benefits and SLAs you need, and top of that, they can assist you in your day-to-day work also.

Mike Resseler – MVP Hyper-V

Being prepared when a data loss occurs, caused by human error or a technical disaster, is important. Your business needs to continue running after such an incident. Running all, or even the most important, virtual machines is typically a needful resource for your business. This chapter will make you familiar with backup methods for Hyper-V hosts and VMs and continue with Hyper-V Replica as Hyper-V's primary disaster recovery component. You will also learn how to make a Storage Replica and how to automate a complete end-to-end disaster recovery process.

This chapter includes the following topics:

- Hyper-V Replica and extension
- Microsoft Azure Site Recovery
- Windows Server Backup and Hyper-V
- Microsoft Azure Backup
- Storage Replica

Protecting a Hyper-V environment

Preparing for a situation that hopefully never takes place; this is a definition of the process of backup and disaster recovery. While restoring a lost Word document on a file server is a common and well-practiced task occurring daily in most IT environments, the complete loss of a bunch of VMs or even a whole Hyper-V cluster is unlikely to occur; or so you may think. Almost all companies make use of redundant components, and even clusters are standard; however, **single points of failures** (**SPOFs**) can often be found. The following are a few examples:

* Non-mirrored storage systems
* Core switches
* Intersite networking
* Authentication systems

So, a typical technical architecture offers a realistic chance for a disaster to occur. Hardware and software issues aren't number 1 in a list of possible disaster scenarios. More than 50 percent of all disastrous issues are triggered by a human error according to the backup-focused company Acronis. Deleting the wrong VM, provisioning wipe commands against production environments instead of lab systems, mistyping IP addresses, or simply (the classic staff stumbling) over the wrong set of cables happen very fast and very often. In the previous chapter, you learned a lot about HA. You cannot prepare your Hyper-V environment to withstand any kind of problems without a service interruption. You have to decide which disasters to prepare for and which risks you want to take. Let's jump to the point where all your HA efforts have failed, it's disaster time!

Hyper-V Replica

The core feature of Hyper-V disaster recovery technologies is Hyper-V Replica, the ability to replicate a virtual machine in near real time to another Hyper-V host. On the second host, an offline copy of the virtual machine is created and updated every 30 seconds or alternatively, every few minutes, with changed blocks from the running source-VM. Both physical machines host nearly identical copies of the same virtual machine with the same name, the same IP address, and the same content. Optional VSS consistency provides additional data integrity throughout the replication process. The replicated VM is offline until a disaster takes place and the VM will be powered up (manually) when it's needed. Both hosts don't have to use identical hardware, storage systems, or Active Directory domains. Instead of restoring up to 24-hour-old data from your backup, the maximum data loss in this scenario is only a few minutes of data.

In the case of a broken SAN, you will decrease the time to return to production from your old timeframe:

- **Identify the problem**: 30 minutes
- **SAN Replacement SLA**: 8 hours
- **Restore terabytes of data from the Tier 2 backup archive**: 48 hours

Just power on the virtual machines on the replica host, and after their boot is completed you are back in production. The replication between the virtual machines is automatically reversed. All changes to your virtual machine in a disaster situation are replicated back to the source VM when it becomes available again. After restoring the primary hardware, wait for the replication to complete and switch back in a controlled process to the primary systems. This process will need a short downtime but will occur without data loss.

You can replicate between standalone hosts, between clusters, and even between standalone hosts and a cluster. You cannot replicate between hosts that are members of the same cluster because the replica virtual machine is an exact copy of the original, and you cannot have duplicates within the cluster. Hyper-V Replica is an ideal candidate to be considered for data redundancy and disaster compute resources. If possible, place the Replica hosts on another site or even another geographic region. It's possible to replicate to another datacenter or to Microsoft's public cloud over WAN. There are several automation options available for Hyper-V Replica, that is, PowerShell and Azure Site Recovery (both are covered in this chapter), as well as System Center 2016 with its Orchestrator Component (covered in `Chapter 8`, *Management with System Center and Azure*).

It's a best practice to use slower/older hardware and cheaper storage architecture on Replica sites when they are only used as Replica targets. If you have nonproduction systems such as development or lab-VMs, move them to your Replica targets and shut them down in a disaster scenario. If you have identical hardware setups on both sides, host VMs on both sites and configure crossover replication between the hosts.

Hyper-V Replica is not a backup solution; it is a disaster recovery plan solution. The VMs are replicated nearly synchronously. If a corruption occurs in the source VM, the corruption will be also replicated. With Hyper-V Replica, you can't keep recovery points for the previous day. The maximum number of replicas is 24 for a full day only. If you need a backup solution, refer to the *Backup of virtual machines* section.

Enabling Hyper-V Replica

To enable Hyper-V Replica for your existing virtual machines, we follow a five-step process as shown here:

- Prepare the first host for sending replication data and receiving data in a disaster scenario
- Enable the Replica hosts to receive replication data and send data in a disaster scenario
- Activate replication on selected virtual machines and configure the replication scenario
- Monitor the replication
- Test Hyper-V Replica

Preparing the first host

Our Hyper-V installation does not allow the replication of virtual machines by default and Hyper-V Replica needs to be enabled.

Start an elevated PowerShell and execute the following command:

```
Set-VMReplicationServer –AllowedAuthenticationType kerberos –
    –ReplicationEnabled 1
```

To enable this on multiple hosts, use and also set the default location for incoming replications:

```
Set-VMReplicationServer –AllowedAuthenticationType kerberos –`
    ReplicationEnabled 1
    –ComputerName "Pyhyv01", "Pyhyv02"
    –DefaultStorageLocation
"C:\ClusterStorage\Volume1\Hyper–V Replica"
```

The default authentication method used with Hyper-V Replica is Kerberos. Use Kerberos in an already secured environment if all participating hosts are joined to the same Active Directory domain. If you are replicating over WAN connections or have different domains (Replica is truly independent of Active Directory domains), switch to certificate-based authentication, which also adds encrypted data transfers:

```
Set-VMReplicationServer -ReplicationEnabled 1
    -AllowedAuthenticationType Certificate
    -CertificateAuthenticationPort 8000
    -CertificateThumbprint
"0442C676C8726ADDD1CE029AFC20EB158490AFC8"
```

Replace the certificate thumbprint with the corresponding one from the certificate you want to use. The equivalent certificate with its private key must be present on all involved hosts. Use an existing trusted certificate authority to create the certificates and GPOs to distribute them to the corresponding hosts. Use a certificate template for server authentication when issuing certificates to your Hyper-V hosts. Use the server's FQDN as the subject name. However, if no existing CA is available or can be set up, I recommend that you use *Makecert* to create a self-signed certificate quickly and easily. Obtain the tool and the instructions to create self-signed certificates for Hyper-V Replica at https://blogs.technet.microsoft.com/virtualization/2013/04/13/hyper-v-replica-certificate-based-authentication-makecert/.

If you are using Hyper-V hosts in a Failover Cluster, the replica configuration is only needed once per cluster. To achieve this, create a Hyper-V Replica Broker role via elevated PowerShell:

```
Add-ClusterServerRole -Name Replica-Broker -StaticAddress 192.168.1.5
Add-ClusterResource -Name "Virtual Machine Replication Broker"
    -Type "Virtual Machine Replication Broker"
    -Group Replica-Broker
Add-ClusterResourceDependency "Virtual Machine Replication Broker"
Replica-
Broker
Start-ClusterGroup Replica-Broker
```

Keep in mind that, when using certificate-based authentication, you need to issue additional certificates with the FQDN of the Hyper-V Broker role to all Hyper-V hosts. To enable successful replications to our hosts later on, we need to prepare the running Windows Firewall. Do this via GPO or run the following PowerShell script once in a cluster for Kerberos-based authentication:

```
get-clusternode | ForEach-Object  {Invoke-command -computername $_.name
-
scriptblock {Enable-Netfirewallrule -displayname "Hyper-V Replica HTTP
```

```
Listener (TCP-In)"}}
```

Also, run the following script for certificate-based authentication:

```
get-clusternode | ForEach-Object  {Invoke-command –computername $_.name

scriptblock {Enable-Netfirewallrule –displayname "Hyper-V Replica HTTPS
Listener (TCP-In)"}}
```

By default, Hyper-V Replica allows incoming replications from all servers. It's a best practice to filter this to only the corresponding replication hosts. First, enable selective replication as follows:

```
Set-VMReplicationServer –AllowedAuthenticationType kerberos –
ReplicationEnabled 1 –ComputerName "Pyhyv01", "Pyhyv02" –
DefaultStorageLocation "C:\ClusterStorage\Volume1\Hyper-V Replica"–
ReplicationAllowedFromAnyServer 0
```

Then, use the following:

```
New-VMReplicationAuthorizationEntry –AllowedPrimaryServer
Pyhyv01.int.homecloud.net
-ReplicaStorageLocation C:\ClusterStorage\Volume1\
-TrustGroup EYGroup01
-ComputerName Pyhyv02.int.homecloud.net
```

Here, `TrustGroup` is a logical group. Add all corresponding replication hosts and brokers to the same security tag. You can use wildcard characters for a particular domain without having to specify all hosts individually (for example, `*.elanity.com`).

After that, our first Hyper-V host or cluster is ready to use Hyper-V Replica.

Preparing additional hosts

Repeat the steps for additional hosts, if you are using a more standalone Hyper-V server. Make sure you use consistent trust groups/security tags.

The GUI should reflect your changes as shown in the following screenshot:

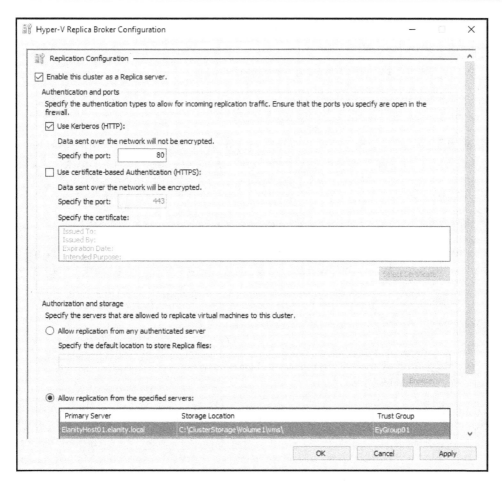

Hyper-V replica configuration

Activate VM replication

The replication of VMs is configured on a per-VM basis; typically, you select all production VMs for replication. Keep using PowerShell to configure this efficiently.

Run the following PowerShell cmdlets from an elevated Shell to replicate the VM01 virtual machine to the pyhyv02 host:

```
Set-VMReplication -VMName VM01
    -ReplicaServerName pyhyv02.int.homecloud.net `
    -ReplicaServerPort 80
```

This is all the configuration needed to prepare the replication. Start the initial replication by executing the following command:

```
Start-VMInitialReplication -VMName VM01
```

The replication is started and all set to go. However, there is a great set of recommended options to customize the replica configuration.

By adding `-CompressionEnabled 1`, all the replication traffic gets compressed before its replication occurs. The very small amount of CPU cycles needed to compress and extract the packets is a great trade-off for a lot of expensive bandwidth saving and is highly recommended:

```
Start-VMInitialReplication -VMName VM01 -CompressionEnabled 1
```

The initial replication can be a huge amount of data. To not overwhelm the network or WAN bandwidth, it can be scheduled to occur at a specific time by adding the following:

```
-InitialReplicationStartTime 5/1/2014 7:00 AM
```

A great parameter I recommend that you add is as follows:

```
Set-VMReplication –VMName VM01 `
    -ReplicaServerName Pyhyv02.int.homecloud.net `
    -RecoveryHistory 24
```

This ensures that not only the current replica of the virtual machine is stored on the replica server but also the last 24 Versions of the virtual machine. This is incredibly useful if the primary VMs are hit by a logical error such as a computer virus. The virus will be replicated near real time into your disaster-ready VMs. Just power off the source VMs and reboot an older recovery point, that is, 2 hours back in time, where you are sure the virus is not yet present. In this way, you can recover from a destructive computer virus or human error in minutes instead of days.

Set the replication frequency to 30, 300, or 900 seconds. I recommend that you use 30 seconds as a default value for the first 50 VMs. When replicating more than 50 VMs, switch to 300 seconds as your default, because of increased system resources used for replication. If one replication window is missed or the replica window needs longer than your replication interval, it will continue with the next available replication window:

```
-ReplicationFrequencySec 30
```

To ensure application consistency, add regular VSS snapshots to our replication by adding the following:

```
-VSSSnapshotFrequencyHour 4
```

This will ensure that VSS snapshots occur every 4 hours.

The final PowerShell Script should look like the following script:

```
    Set-VMReplication -VMName VM01 -ReplicaServerName
Pyhyv02.int.homecloud.net -ReplicaServerPort 80
    -RecoveryHistory 24 -ReplicationFrequencySec 30 -
VSSSnapshotFrequencyHour 4
    Start-VMInitialReplication -VMName VM01 -CompressionEnabled 1 -
InitialReplicationStartTime 5/1/2014
    7:00 AM
```

Activate this for the virtual machines you want to protect for disaster recovery.

It is a best practice to move temporary files to a different virtual hard disk and exclude it from replication to save bandwidth and ensure fast replication times. The Windows pagefile is a great example of a temp file not needed on the replica site. There is a great TechNet blogpost on this topic. For details, refer to `https://blogs.technet.microsoft.com/virtu alization/2014/05/11/excluding-virtual-disks-in-hyper-v-replica/`.

Hyper-V Replica is fully compatible with Windows Server Network Virtualization and its Quality of Service settings. It's a great way to throttle Replica traffic during peak office hours. Refer to `Chapter 5`, *Network Best Practices*, for details.

The configuration shown to implement Hyper-V Replica can also be done in the GUI of Windows Server. However, for scaling purposes, you should prefer PowerShell. To automate the whole process, use the following script to configure Hyper-V Replica between two hosts:

```
    $HVSource = "Pyhyv01"
    $HVReplica = "Pyhyv02"
    $Port = 80
    $HVdisabld = get-vm -ComputerName $HVSource | where
{$_.replicationstate -eq
    'disabled' }
    foreach ($VM in $HVdisabld) {
    enable-VMReplication $VM $Replica $Port $Auth
    Set-VMReplication -VMName $VM.name  -ReplicaServerName $HVReplica -
    ReplicaServerPort $Port -AuthenticationType kerberos -
CompressionEnabled $true
    -RecoveryHistory 0 -computername $HVSource
    Start-VMInitialReplication $VM.name  -ComputerName $HVSource
```

Monitoring Hyper-V Replica

Use `Measure-VMReplication | format-list *` to get details of the current replication processes. Use System Center Operations Manager for a complete health monitoring of Hyper-V Replica, as follows:

```
Name                            : contoso2
Id                              : 61388695-555a-49d2-9f14-26886eca9edb
State                           : Replicating
Health                          : Normal
LRep17ime                       : 18-3-2012 15:24:24
PReplSize                       : 4096
AvgLatency                      : 00:01:07
AvgReplSize                     : 5369016576
SuccReplCount                   : 2
CurrentTask                     : {}
MonitoringStartTime             : 18-3-2012 15:06:28
MonitoringEndTime               : 18-3-2012 15:25:42
LastReplicationType             : None
FailedOverReplicationType       : None
LastTestFailoverInitiatedTime   :
LastVSSSnapshotTime             :
InitialReplicationSize          : 0
PendingReplicationSize          : 4096
AverageReplicationSize          : 5369016576
MaximumReplicationSize          : 10736369664
AverageReplicationLatency       : 00:01:07
MaximumReplicationLatency       : 00:02:15
ReplicationErrors               : 0
SuccessfulReplicationCount      : 2
MissedReplicationCount          : 0
ComputerName                    : VMHOST2
PrimaryServerName               : VMHOST2.contoso.com
CurrentReplicaServerName        : vmhost1.contoso.com
ReplicaServerName               : vmhost1.contoso.com
ReplicationState                : Replicating
ReplicationHealth               : Normal
ReplicationMode                 : Primary
LastReplicationTime             : 18-3-2012 15:24:24
ReplicatedDisks                 : (Hard Drive on IDE controller number 0 at location 0)
SecurityTag                     :
TestVirtualMachine              :
VMId                            : 61388695-555a-49d2-9f14-26886eca9edb
VMName                          : contoso2
IsDeleted                       : False
```

Monitor the state of Hyper-V Replica

Hyper-V Replica testing and failover

There are multiple options to test whether your replica is working. Execute a planned failover for switching one VM without data loss to the replica node. Be aware, this involves a short downtime of the VM:

```
Stop-VM -VMName VM1 -ComputerName Pyhyv01
Start-VMFailover -VMName VM01 -ComputerName Pyhyv01
-Prepare
```

The preceding command stops the original VMs and prepares both hosts for a planned failover. Execute the following command to force a planned failover:

```
Start-VMFailover -VMName VM01 -ComputerName Pyhyv02
-as Test
```

If your disaster takes place, just remove `-as Test` to start the real failover, and reverse the replication with the following:

```
Set-VMReplication -VMName  VM01 -ComputerName Pyhyv02
-Reverse
```

The question I get asked most often is how to automate this failover process. I strongly recommend that you do only manual failovers to avoid split-brain situations, where the same VM is powered on accidentally on both sites. However, for scripting, this in an on-premise situation. For more details, refer to `https://blogs.technet.microsoft.com/keit` `hmayer/2012/10/05/automated-disaster-recovery-testing-and-failover-with-hype` `r-v-replica-and-powershell-3-0-for-free/` or use the Azure Site Recovery service covered later in this chapter.

Another great way to test your replica is to do a test failover. This creates a copy of selected virtual machines in an isolated environment without affecting the production service. This way, you can test the replicated VM without any time constraints. Refer to `https://blogs.` `technet.microsoft.com/virtualization/2012/07/25/types-of-failover-operations` `-in-hyper-v-replica-part-i-test-failover/` for more information on different failover types.

In a testing scenario or at a disaster site, it may be necessary to alter the IP configuration of the replicated virtual machines due to other subnets being used at that site:

```
Set-VMNetworkAdapterFailoverConfiguration VM01'
    -IPv4Address 192.168.1.1
    -IPv4SubnetMask 255.255.255.0
    -IPv4DefaultGateway 192.168.1.254
```

To change the vSwitch of the VM for a test failover, use the following:

```
Set-VMNetworkAdapter âVM01'
-TestReplicaSwitchName 'vSwitchTest01'
```

Have a look at the GUI representation of these options in the following screenshot:

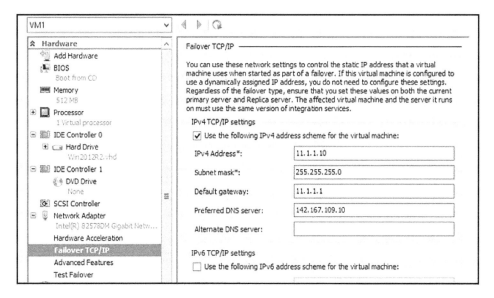

Failover TCP/IP address of the replicated VM

After configuring these options, you are all set for widespread disaster recovery with Hyper-V Replica. You can even configure your replica VM to extend another replication to a third site, for instance, a partner datacenter.

Azure Site Recovery

With Azure Site Recovery, Microsoft offers a complete end-to-end solution. Install two Hyper-V hosts as you learned in the previous chapters, do not cluster them, but add them to one or two instances of System Center Virtual Machine Manager 2012/2012 R2/2016.

Log on to a **Microsoft Azure** subscription, use a trial subscription if you have none, and create a new **Backup** and **Site Recovery** vault that will host all replica-related information. Refer to `https://azure.microsoft.com/fr-fr/documentation/articles/site-recover y-vmm-to-azure/` for details. You also need a storage account and a virtual network located in the same location as the backup and site recovery vault. To make a disaster recovery plan in Azure you need to install the Azure Site Recovery Provider on your SCVMM Server and install the Azure Recovery Services Agent on each Hyper-V host. Refer to `http://www.tech -coffee.net/protect-hyper-v-vm-microsoft-azure-azure-site-recovery/` for details:

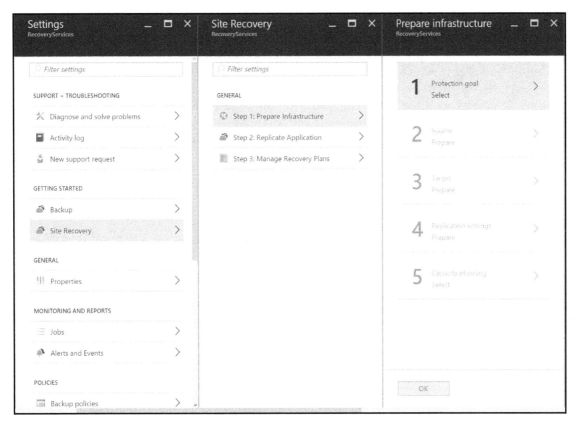

Azure Site Recovery from Azure Portal

You can now control these hosts through Microsoft's public cloud, Microsoft Azure. With Azure Site Recovery, you can enable Hyper-V Replica, configure its authentication and replication options, and select groups of VMs (SCVMM louds). All the selected virtual machines will be enabled for Hyper-V Replica automatically and you can even set options for automatic failover processes. In this case, only the orchestration and management are done through Microsoft Azure. You can now even select Microsoft Azure as a storage target for Hyper-V Replica. Incoming network traffic to Azure is free, so this is a very cost-effective solution compared to building another datacenter to host backup systems.

Once you have replicated VM into Microsoft Azure, you can map your on-premise networks used by virtual machines to the corresponding Azure networks. Then you can build and test recovery plans. The recovery plan enables you to build logical groups of VMs to define the order in which VMs start, including a slight delay between the groups so that you can start your Active Directory before your database servers and start your ERP Server after all databases are online. You can also add manual tasks and some automations between each groups of VMs to verify and automate tasks. A virtual machine is only built from the replicated storage data when there is an emergency and a failover to Azure occurs. Welcome to a real hybrid cloud scenario!

Replica workloads

Before you now start to mirror all your virtual machines at a cost, keep in mind that your workload needs to be able to handle the failover mechanisms of Hyper-V Replica. Hyper-V Replica requires all applications running inside replicated VMs to be able to handle an unplanned power-off of the VM, because this is exactly what happens in an unplanned failover scenario. Most applications have no problem with this, including the current versions of Windows Server Domain Controllers hosting Active Directory and Microsoft SQL Servers. Other applications such as Microsoft's Lync or Exchange Server are currently not supported in conjunction with Hyper-V Replica. Both applications however do provide great application-specific HA and DR mechanisms that should be leveraged instead.

Storage Replica

Storage Replica is a new feature in Windows Server 2016 and provides block replication from a storage level for a data recovery plan or for a stretched cluster. Storage Replica can be used in the following scenarios:

- Server-to-server storage replication using Storage Replica
- Storage replication in a stretch cluster using Storage Replica
- Cluster-to-cluster storage replication using Storage Replica
- Server-to-itself to replicate between volumes using Storage Replica

Regarding the scenario or the bandwidth and the latency of the inter-site link, you can choose between a synchronous and an asynchronous replication. For further information about Storage Replica, you can about read this topic at: https://technet.microsoft.com/ en-us/windows-server-docs/storage/storage-replica/storage-replica-overview.

The SMB3 protocol is used to make Storage Replica. You can leverage TCP/IP or RDMA on the network. I recommend you implement RDMA when possible to reduce latency and CPU workload and to increase throughput.

Compared to Hyper-V Replica, the Storage Replica feature provides a replication of all Virtual Machines stored in a volume from the block level. Moreover, Storage Replica can replicate in synchronous mode while Hyper-V Replica is always in asynchronous mode. To finish, with Hyper-V Replica you have to specify the failover IP Address because the replication is executed from the VM level, whereas with Storage Replica you don't need to specify the failover IP Address; however in the case of a replication between two clusters in two different rooms, the VM networks must be configured in the destination room.

The use of Hyper-V Replica or Storage Replica depends on the disaster recovery plan you need. If you want to protect some application workloads, you can use Hyper-V Replica. On the other hand, if you have the passive room ready to restart in case of issues in the active room, Storage Replica can be a great solution because all the VMs in a volume will be already replicated.

To deploy a replication between two clusters you need two sets of storage based on iSCSI, SAS JBOD, fibre channel SAN, or Shared VHDX. For better performance I recommend you implement SSD, which will be used for the logs of Storage Replica.

To enable Storage Replica, execute the following steps:

1. Install the required features on each server:

```
Install-WindowsFeature Storage-Replica, Failover-Clustering
    -IncludeManagementTools
    -ComputerName HV01, HV02, HV03, HV04 -Restart
```

2. Create the clusters as shown in the `Chapter 2`, *Deploying Highly Available Hyper-V Clusters*.

3. In each cluster, at least two LUNs are necessary for the data and logs. Logs and replicated volumes must have the same size in both clusters. The logs volume is mapped on `L`:

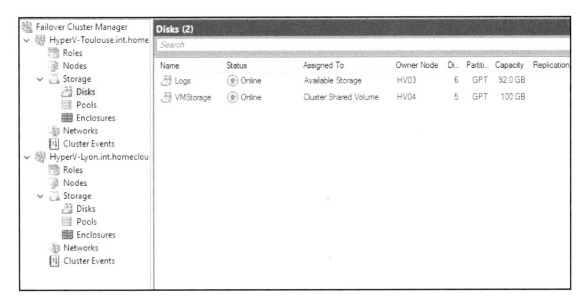

Disks configuration in both clusters

4. Grant Storage Replica access from the first cluster to the second and vice versa:

```
Grant-SRAccess -ComputerName hv01 -Cluster hyperv-toulouse
Grant-SRAccess -ComputerName hv03 -Cluster hyperv-lyon
```

5. Enable Storage Replica with the partner:

```
New-SRPartnership -SourceComputerName Hyperv-Lyon `
                  -SourceRGName VMGroup01 `
                  -SourceVolumeName C:\ClusterStorage\volume1 `
                  -SourceLogVolumeName L: `
                  -DestinationCOmputerName HyperV-Toulouse `
                  -DestinationRGName VMGroup02 `
                  -DestinationVolumeName C:\ClusterStorage\Volume1 `
                  -DestinationLogVolumeName L:
```

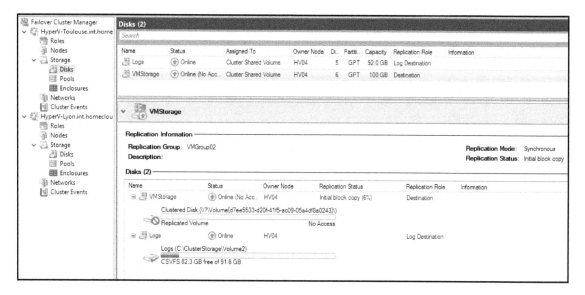

Volumes on the destination cluster

Now, if the site located in Lyon has trouble, you can delete the replication to access the data located in the destination replicated volume:

```
Remove-SRPartnership -DestinationComputerName HyperV-Toulouse
    -SourceComputerName Hyper-V-Lyon
    -SourceRGName VMGroup01
    -DestinationRGName VMGroup02
    -IgnoreRemovalFail
Remove-SRGroup -ComputerName HyperV-Toulouse -Name VMGroup02
```

Backup of virtual machines

A disaster recovery solution such as Hyper-V Replica or Storage Replica protects you from a lot of catastrophic scenarios; however, it's not a substitute for a successful backup. Hyper-V backup solutions shifted away from the classic grandfather-father-son backup schedule with nightly backups of every system. Modern Hyper-V backup solutions such as Microsoft's Data Protection Manager work host-based on a block level and track every change happening to any VM included in a backup. These changes are saved as an incremental, continual backup running every 15 minutes. These ensure a quick backup, a fast restore, and reduce data loss in the case of a recovery to a maximum of 15 minutes. Most **Recovery Point Objectives (RPOs)** and **Recovery Time Objectives (RTOs)** backup SLAs can be met easily with a powerful backup tool. Be careful and choose only a backup tool that is specifically tested with Windows Server 2016 Hyper-V and Cluster Shared Volumes/SMB3 shares. Today, there are many backup solutions on the market that are not capable of this, including the former market leader of infrastructure backup.

After you have implemented your backup tool successfully, make sure you test the recovery of virtual machines on a regular basis. It is very important that it works so that you keep your backup software with the latest patch like every other component in your Hyper-V environment.

For a successful backup, it's very important that your VSS providers are working and that the integration services of every VM are up to date. To ensure successful backup solutions, make sure you have as few Hyper-V checkpoints enabled on your VMs as possible. A huge chain of checkpoints does endanger the integrity of a running VM and its backups. Also, it's still the best practice to keep a set of backups offsite in case of a real disaster. Here, an interesting option comes into play, because a Hyper-V Replica-protected VM produces an exact copy of the VM, but powered off, which is a great source for backups. Without affecting the production environment and without any VSS-related problems, taking backups from the Replica-VM simplifies offsite backups as well as branch office scenarios. Simply replicate VMs from your branch office to your central datacenter and include the Replica VMs in your primary backup.

For smaller environments, even the Windows Server Backup (`wbadmin.exe`) is capable of running host-based Hyper-V backups. Windows Server Backup needs to be enabled first before it can be used. Run the following PowerShell cmdlet to enable wbadmin from an elevated prompt:

```
Add-WindowsFeature Windows-Server-Backup
```

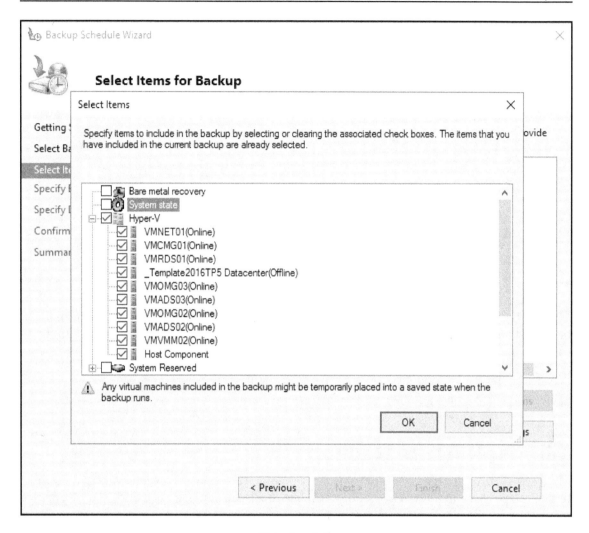

Windows Server Backup

To back up a single virtual machine, just use the following command:

```
wbadmin start backup –backupTarget:d:–hyperv:VM01 –force
```

This enables backing up the `VM01` VM to the local `D:` of the host. The VM will stay online during the process as long as current integration services are being used. The `-force` parameter starts the backup immediately without waiting for manual confirmations. wbadmin is capable of storing multiple backups for the same VM when using local storage as a backup target. You can also use network shares as the backup target, but old backups will be overwritten.

To restore a backup with wbadmin, you first need to identify the exact date and time of the backup, since it marks the backup version:

```
wbadmin get versions -backupTarget:d:
```

Copy the version identifier shown for your backups and use it in the following command:

```
wbadmin start recover-version:08/18/2014-22:01 -itemType: hyperv
âitems:VM01âbackuptarget:d:
```

This restores the `VM01` VM from backup location `D:` with the identified version.

You can backup and restore multiple VMs via wbadmin by a comma separating VM names or virtual machine IDs. Even if you don't have the need to restore your VMs on a regular basis, be sure you test your backups now and then.

A full command-line reference for `wbadmin` is available at `https://technet.microsoft.com/en-us/library/cc754015.aspx`.

Microsoft Azure Backup

Microsoft Azure provides a solution to back up your workloads to an external site. Instead of using tape disks in a library for long-term backups, you can use the cloud. A best practice for backups is the *3-2-1* rule, which is a follows:

- **3** copies of the data (including the source location)
- **2** different storage devices
- **1** copy on an extra site

Microsoft Azure Backup helps us to follow this best practice easily. When using this feature, you make a short-term backup on a local disk and a long-term backup in Azure. In this way you have two copies of the data in your datacenter and one in the Cloud. Thanks to Microsoft Azure, you have the different storage device and the extra site.

As for Azure Site Recovery, you need to create a backup and site recovery vault. If you do not have System Center **Data Protection Manager** (**DPM**), I recommend you use Azure Server Backup. This software is the same as DPM except that you can't back up to tape disks. Azure Server Backup is free and can be downloaded from the Azure Portal:

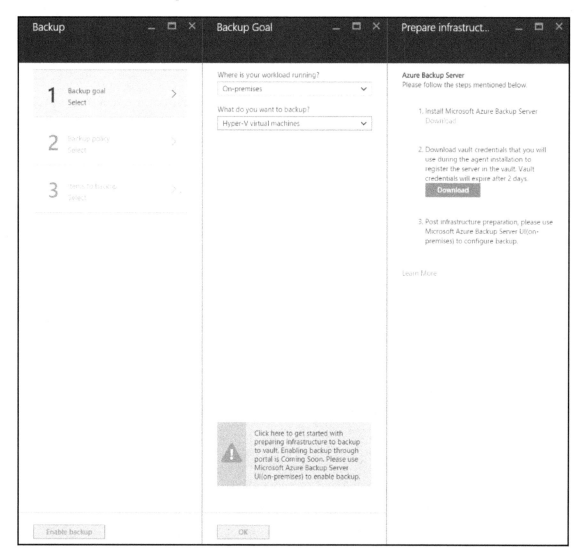

Azure Backup from Azure Portal

Once you have created the backup and site recovery vault, you can follow these steps to back up Hyper-V VM:

1. Install Azure Backup Server and use the vault credentials during this installation process.
2. Add available disks to Azure Backup Server for short-term backup usage.
3. Install the Azure Backup Server agent on Hyper-V Server. You can find the agent in the following location on the Azure Backup Server (default location):

```
C:\Program Files\Microsoft Azure
Backup\DPM\DPM\ProtectionAgents\RA\11.0.50.0\amd64\DPMAgentInstaller_x64.ex
e
```

4. Connect them to the Azure Backup Server:

```
C:\Program Files\Microsoft Data Protection Manager\DPM\bin\SetDPMServer

DPMServerName <MyAzureBackupServer>
```

5. Add the agents of each Hyper-V node in the cluster to Azure Backup Server.
6. Create a protection group, select Hyper-V VMs, and choose short-term backup on disk and long-term backup on Cloud. Configure the backup policy as required.

Summary

You now know that HA and disaster recovery are two completely different and independent architectures. You can now leverage the best of both worlds and protect your Hyper-V environment from common disasters, via manual configuration, PowerShell scripting, or through end-to-end solutions such as Azure Site Recovery or Azure Backup.

With your knowledge about backup architectures and tools, you are able to secure your virtual machine content even in the event of a huge disaster.

Continue now to `Chapter 4`, *Storage Best Practices*, to learn more about the great new storage options provided by Windows Server 2016 and Hyper-V.

4
Storage Best Practices

The Windows High Available Fileserver (commonly called Scale-Out Fileserver), Storage Spaces, and of course SMB3 are three great new technologies that are really promising and work great with Hyper-V. I personally think that the legacy of classic SAN storage systems is over because Software Defined Storage solutions are much more flexible and not nearly as expensive as SAN solutions. So prepare yourself to play/test these new solutions!
Carsten Rachfahl – MVP Hyper-V

This chapter will familiarize you with the common storage architectures that are compatible with Hyper-V and how to use them most efficiently. With Windows Server 2016 and Hyper-V, the storage landscape for virtualization changed dramatically. For the earlier versions of Windows Server, an expensive SAN was required for high performance cluster systems. As of today, many alternatives are available for cost-efficient, high performance, and HA Hyper-V Storage sizing and technologies.

These are the topics we'll be covering in this chapter:

- Hyper-V disk formats and types
- SAN versus Storage Spaces
- Disaggregated and hyperconverged solutions
- Storage Spaces and tiering
- iSCSI target server
- Deduplication and thin provisioning
- ReFS and Hyper-V
- Storage QoS policies

Storage overview

Storage for Hyper-V is not primarily about capacity; it is about performance. Stop thinking in terms of capacities such as gigabytes and terabytes of data and calculate in IOPS from now on when Hyper-V Storage options are on the table. Of course, you still need to make sure there is enough capacity available. However, these typically neither influence the design nor the costs on a larger scale since high capacity hard drives are available for a very low price. There are very different approaches for a virtualization storage design.

In older versions of Windows Server and other virtualization products, a NAS system for smaller environments and enterprise-grade SAN systems were used as a storage backend. With a Fibre Channel or iSCSI connection to the Virtualization Server Systems, it provides a central storage for all nodes in a cluster, ensuring capabilities such as VM live migration and Cluster Failover.

The loss of cluster nodes does not impact the integrity and availability of the storage systems. The **Logical Unit Numbers** (**LUNs**) of SAN/NAS systems appear as local drives on the Hyper-V hosts. Traditional architectures came with a one-VM-per-LUN approach, which was dropped in modern approaches for Cluster shared volumes that host multiple VMs per LUN. SAN systems of NAS systems for small Hyper-V setups are still the most frequently used storage architecture around these days and are fully supported by the recent version of Hyper-V. The use of cluster shared volumes has been improved a lot and is the default deployment option for storage volumes for Hyper-V on a SAN.

A more modern approach is the use of the onboard capabilities of Windows Server storage management. Leveraging the SMB3 performance and availability options of Storage Spaces with attached **just a bunch of disks** (**JBODs**) or direct attached storage devices allows you to generate IOPS for Hyper-V on a large scale for a considerably lower price. Microsoft Storage Spaces allows you to utilize the best features you know from a SAN with just one or more physical server systems running Windows Server. You can use traditional storage LUNs behind **Scale-Out File Servers** (**SOFS**) or use Storage Spaces with hard drives connected to the storage nodes. These hard drives are connected through the system as **JBOD** or attached internally to the system without the use of a hardware RAID controller.

Availability on the storage level is done on a software level by Windows Server. Storage Spaces offers scalable performance; it is not just a small business solution. VMs are no longer placed on LUNs; instead, they leverage Storage Spaces and cluster shared volume. We will see later in this chapter that the two models exist now in Windows Server 2016 to implement software-defined storage for Hyper-V-the disaggregated and hyperconverged models.

The disaggregated model leverages SOFS with several file servers. These file servers can be connected to traditional shared JBOD or with internal storage devices by using Storage Spaces Direct. On the other hand, in the hyperconverged model, hypervisors are also storage nodes. Hypervisors are connected to storage devices, either JBOD or internally to the system, and leverage Storage Spaces Direct to make the storage layer highly available (we will discuss Storage Spaces Direct later in this chapter).

For both solutions, there is no need for expensive SANs or even a RAID controller to achieve high availability and good performance. Storage Spaces builds a full storage virtualization abstraction of the connected disks that are even capable of automatically tiering used SSDs and classic hard drives in the same JBODs for optimal performance.

Of course, Hyper-V can also leverage local hard disks in a server system for the storage of VMs. The VMs can even be replicated to another Hyper-V host in terms of disaster recovery like you learned in `Chapter 3`, *Backup and Disaster Recovery*, but they do not offer HA capabilities and should therefore not be used in production.

SANs versus Storage Spaces

One of the most crucial decisions in a storage design process for Hyper-V is the question of whether to stick with the traditional SAN model or hop on the wagon of Microsoft's Storage Spaces architecture. Both solutions can do the main job, that is, providing IOPS for VMs without any problems. Having done many projects using both architectures, the following is some real-world guidance I use for storage design.

The first and most important design principle is: do not use nonredundant systems in production for Hyper-V clusters-no single hardware storage node and no single point of failures in your storage design. If you cannot fulfill these requirements, don't plan for HA on Hyper-V. Plan for disaster recovery instead. Uncluster the Hyper-V Servers and replicate the VMs between the nodes in a small setup or between smaller clusters in a bigger environment via Hyper-V Replica. Having said that, let's focus on the decision to make.

Technically, it's possible to use a SOFS in conjunction with a SAN. However, with SAN vendors adapting SMB3 protocols, this is not an efficient long-term scenario in most cases, and we will focus on using Storage Spaces with shared JBOD and Storage Spaces Direct with direct-attached storage. There are some SOFS architectures with a SAN you should leverage, particularly, for Fibre Channel SANs, where the Hyper-V hosts may only have Ethernet adapters. Leveraging the SOFS as the entry point to the storage environment reduces the configuration complexity of the compute nodes by placing all the storage vendor requirements on the storage nodes of the SOFS cluster. You can also place several SANs behind a single SOFS cluster and provide a consistent management and storage presentation experience across the virtualization platform, which will allow you to deploy any variety of storage vendor hardware. However, most of the time with Windows Server 2016, when you want go with Storage Spaces, the hard drives will be located in the shared JBOD or be directly attached to the storage nodes and no longer in a SAN.

While SAN systems have been around for 15 years, Storage Spaces has only been around since Windows Server 2012. If you are working in a large company and have enabled a SAN architecture through your company, including all different applications, operating systems, and requirements, stick with SANs. If you have maintained a uniform storage architecture through all these different areas and have proven processes built around it, do not change this for Hyper-V. Make sure that you use Hyper-V-ready SANs with Fibre Channel or iSCSI and continue using them.

In all other design approaches, start under the initial plan of using Storage Spaces. If you find any reason not to use it, switch to a SAN-based solution, but your primary approach should involve Storage Spaces because of its lower price. Don't worry about performance. Storage Spaces is able to provide more than a million IOPS over 10 Gbe-NICs, if you really need it (http://bit.ly/2aOgNTK). Storage Spaces offer Active/Active Cluster configurations leveraging the performance of all storage cluster nodes with the additional benefit of transparent failover. All this is done with Windows Server 2016 capabilities; no third-party additions are necessary. That being said, this is also managed by Windows Server, involving all of the well-known management tools such as Server-Manager and PowerShell. It's way easier to integrate Storage Spaces in an existing Microsoft environment than a SAN, and a lot easier to manage Storage Spaces than a SAN.

The reasons for not using Storage Spaces in a more detailed design process are the advanced requirements. Storage Spaces provides you with bare storage for Hyper-V and SQL databases. If you need storage for other purposes, another operating system, or extra capabilities on the storage level, such as deduplication for server usage, then Storage Spaces is not the right solution for you.

If you want a cheap and fast Windows-based storage solution with SAN-like capabilities, including data deduplication, thin provisioning, and hardware **Offloaded Data Transfer (ODX)**, you are on the right track with Microsoft Storage Spaces. However, if you are currently using a SAN and it does not offer SMB3 capabilities, it may be a good option to use a SOFS in conjunction with the existing SAN.

Having chosen one storage architecture, let's now focus on the best practice configurations of Hyper-V technologies.

NTFS versus Resilient File System (ReFS)

Before talking about Storage Spaces, I'd like to discuss ReFS. Currently Hyper-V supports two filesystems, the classic NTFS, and the more recent Resilient File System (ReFS). Before Windows Server 2016, I recommended that you use NTFS, because ReFS had a lack of some key capabilities and most backup applications have problems with it. Now in Windows Server 2016, Microsoft brings a lot of new features in ReFSv2 as the Accelerated VHDX Operations. The capability enables us to accelerate operations during the following scenarios:

- Creating and extending a virtual hard disk
- Merging checkpoints
- Backups, which are based on production checkpoints (we will discuss production checkpoints later in this chapter)

When you extended a VHD(X) located in an NTFS partition, the system was written by zeroing out the new block. In ReFS, the new blocks are metadata instead. Thanks to ReFS, now you just need between 1 to 5 seconds to create a big VHDX instead of many minutes as in NTFS.

The other advantage of ReFS is related to checkpoints. NTFS copied data from the AVHDX file to the VHDX file. It consumed a lot of time and sometimes, with a checkpoint that existed for a long time, it was impossible to commit. Instead, ReFS merges the AVHDX file with the VHDX file. This results in a fast checkpoint committing.

However, when formatting a CSV in ReFS, this last will work in redirected IO. This means that every IO is sent over the network. This operation doesn't impact performance in Storage Spaces Direct deployment because RDMA adapters are required. But in other deployments, such as using a NAS or a SAN, it can impact the performance deeply.

For all these reasons, I strongly recommend that you use ReFS for VM storage in Windows Server 2016 when you implement Storage Spaces Direct for all others deployments, keep NTFS.

With Hyper-V, it's a best practice to format the volume with 64 KB of block size for optimal performance. The partition alignment is handled automatically, so you don't have to worry about it in the recent Hyper-V versions.

Storage Spaces and tiering

A way to leverage SOFS is to use Storage Spaces with storage tiering. Having some shared JBODs with SSDs and HDDs connected to your SMB3 file servers enables great I/O performance. Frequently read data will be cached on the SSDs and long-term data will be archived on the HDDs by default, without the need for manual editing, which results in a great performance boost. Using the previously explained CSV, a cache can further improve read performance.

With Windows Server 2016, Storage Spaces using shared JBOD should be considered when you already have the hardware (file servers and shared JBOD). If you don't want to invest money in storage because you already have hardware, Storage Spaces with shared JBOD is the way to go. If you plan to buy new hardware, I suggest that you use Storage Spaces Direct which does not require shared JBOD. Shared JBODs are not flexible because they have a limited number of SAS ports. So, the number of file servers is limited by the number of SAS ports on the shared JBOD. Moreover, to ensure HA, two SAS ports should be dedicated to a file server. For example, if you buy a shared JBOD with six SAS ports, you can connect only three file servers. I don't recommend that you use SAS to switch between file servers and shared JBOD for performance reasons.

To create Storage Spaces with tiering through PowerShell, follow these steps:

```
$PhysicalDisks = Get-PhysicalDisk -CanPool $True
New-StoragePool -FriendlyName VMStore01
    -StorageSubsystemFriendlyName"Storage Spaces*"
    -PhysicalDisks $PhysicalDisks
```

Set the SSD and HDD attributes as follows:

```
$tier_ssd = New-StorageTier -StoragePoolFriendlyName VMStore01
    -FriendlyName SSD_TIER
    -MediaType SSD
$tier_hdd = New-StorageTier -StoragePoolFriendlyName VMStore01
    -FriendlyName HDD_TIER
    -MediaType HDD
```

Now you are all set for a great storage space performance that you can use either with SMB3 shares or combined with SOFS.

If you don't want to put all your trust in the (in my opinion, very nicely working) automatic tiering, you can also manually pin frequently accessed files to the SDD tier using the following:

```
Set-FileStorageTier -FilePath d:\Fastfiles\fast.file
    -DesiredStorageTier $tier_ssd
```

Storage Spaces Direct

With Windows Server 2016, we are able to use direct-attached storage devices such as JBOD or internally to the storage nodes to create a highly available storage solution. The storage devices can be connected by either SATA, NVMe, or SAS. The storage devices can be SSD or HDD. To support the high availability, Storage Spaces Direct leverages the Failover Cluster Windows feature.

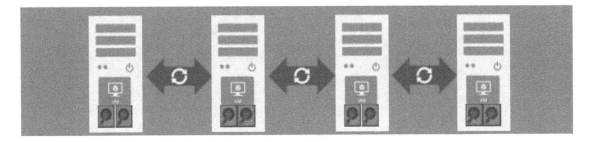

Storage spaces direct with internal disks

A minimum of two nodes is required in the cluster, but not all the Storage Spaces Direct features will be available. To use Multi-Resilient virtual disks (we will discuss it later in this chapter), you need a minimum of four nodes. If you need this feature to gain the maximal performance of this solution, I recommend that you implement at least a four-node cluster. Storage Spaces Direct supports a cluster with a maximum of 16 nodes.

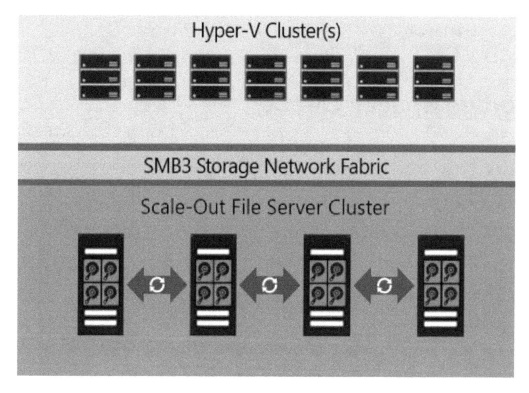

Storage spaces direct leverages failover cluster and SMB protocol

Regarding the network, at least 10 GB/s network adapters are required with **Remote Direct Access Memory (RDMA)**, **DataCenter Bridging (DCB)**, and **Priority Flow Control (PFC)** capabilities. The storage nodes must also support these capabilities where the switches will be connected. RDMA should be either **RDMA over Converged Ethernet (RoCE)** or **internet Wide Area RDMA (iWARP)**. To make network convergence with management networking, live migration or VM networks, I recommend that you use RoCE. Vendors such as Mellanox support these kinds of capabilities really well. I recommend Mellanox from experience, because their network adapters are robust and have great functionalities. Moreover, many Microsoft documentations explain implementation of Mellanox network adapters, so they are well supported by Microsoft.

Unlike Fibre Channel HBA or iSCSI dedicated network adapters, you don't need to install MPIO to support high availability. Instead, Storage Spaces Direct leverages the SMB Multichannel that is auto configured in Windows Server 2016 to use the full bandwidth of each network adapter involved in storage traffics.

If you want to implement the hyperconverged model, Microsoft recommends nodes with at least 128 GB of memory and a dual-socket of modern CPUs such as the Intel Xeon E5 v3 or v4 family. This is because memory and CPU will be leveraged by virtual machines and also for storage needs.

Concerning the storage controllers, you need simple **Host Bus Adapter** (**HBA**) for SAS or SATA devices without RAID functionality. If you use a HBA with RAID functionality, you can degrade performance because the storage controller catches I/O between the operating system and the storage devices.

Storage Spaces direct – disaggregated model

As discussed earlier, Storage Spaces Direct direct can be deployed in the disaggregated model. This means that you implement some file servers with their own storage devices. Then Storage Spaces Direct is used to aggregate storage devices such as HDD or SDD and then create some cluster shared volume to store virtual machines. Because of the use of Storage Spaces Direct, you don't need shared JBOD devices, but you can connect one JBOD per node or use internal storage devices connected by using SATA, SAS, or PCI Express ports.

Once the storage solution is implemented, you deploy SOFS in order that Hyper-V nodes can access storage by using the SMB3 protocol.

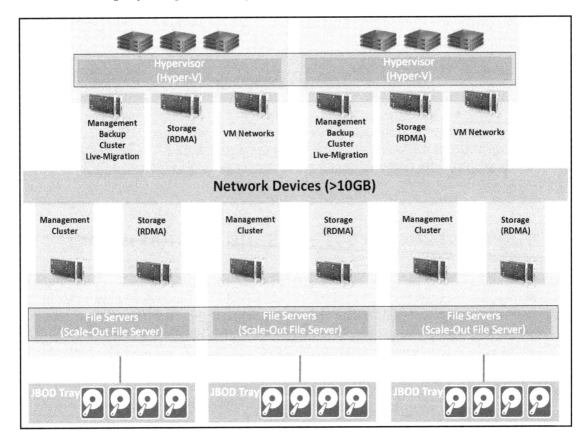

Disaggregated model

You should implement this kind of a solution when you want to independently control the scalability of the storage and computer planes. Adding a node with compute and storage hardware is more expensive than just adding a compute node or a storage node. This solution should be implemented for financial reasons and not for functionality.

Compared to the hyperconverged model, you lose flexibility. You need to be accurate when adding compute nodes to not collapse the storage. In the disaggregated model, the overall performance is divided across Hyper-V nodes. So, when you add a compute node, verify that your storage solution can support this new node in terms of performance and capacity.

To implement this storage solution, just follow these few steps:

1. Spend lot of time on the design to choose storage, networking devices, and architecture.
2. Implement the file server nodes as follows:

   - Install and configure the Windows Server 2016 operating system and the network devices. Flash all firmware to the latest (BIOS, Storage Devices, network controllers, and so on).
   - Install the required features:

```
Install-WindowsFeature FS-FileServer, Failover-Clustering, Data-Center-Bridging, RSAT-Clustering-Mgmt, RSAT-Clustering-Powershell -Restart
```

   - Implement the cluster:

```
Test-Cluster FS01, FS02, FS03, FS04 -Include "Storage Spaces Direct",
Inventory,Network,"System Configuration"
New-Cluster -Name FSCluster`
  -Node FS01, FS02, FS03, FS04 -NoStorage`
  -StaticAddress 10.10.0.164
```

   - Set the cluster Quorum:

```
Set-ClusterQuorum -CloudWitness`
    -Cluster FSCluster`
    -AccountName MyAzureAccount -AccessKey <AccessKey>
```

   - Rename the networks:

```
(Get-ClusterNetwork -Cluster FSCluster -Name "Cluster Network
1").Name="Management"
(Get-ClusterNetwork -Cluster FSCluster -Name "Cluster Network
2").Name="Storage"
(Get-ClusterNetwork -Cluster FSCluster -Name "Cluster Network
3").Name="Cluster"
```

3. Configure the storage as follows:

    -   Enable Storage Spaces Direct:

```
cluster = New-CimSession -ComputerName FSCluster
Enable-ClusterS2D -CimSession $cluster
```

4. Create the Cluster-Shared Volume:

```
New-Volume -StoragePoolFriendlyName S2D* `
        -FriendlyName VMStorage `
        -NumberOfColumns 2 `
        -PhysicalDiskRedundancy 1 `
        -FileSystem CSVFS_REFS `
        -Size 50GB
```

5. Implement Scale-Out file servers as follows:

    -   Deploy the cluster role:

```
Add-ClusterScaleOutFileServerRole -Cluster FSCluster -Name SOFS
```

    -   Create a share:

```
$SharePath = "c:\ClusterStorage\Volume01\VMSTO01"
md $SharePath
New-SmbShare -Name VMSTO01 -Path $SharePath -FullAccess FS01$, FS02$,
FS03$,
    FS04$
Set-SmbPathAcl -ShareName $ShareName
```

Now your file server cluster is ready to store the VHDX virtual machine. When creating a VM from hypervisor, just specify the share path instead of the local storage.

Storage spaces direct: hyperconverged model

Unlike the disaggregated model, the storage devices are placed inside the Hyper-V node themselves. This means that, when you add a node in the cluster, you add compute and storage resources. This solution is great for flexibility, scalability, and automation. The hyperconverged model should be implemented when you want to deploy a private Cloud in your datacenter. Thanks to the flexibility and the simplicity, you can add nodes on demand as almost every Cloud provider.

However, sometimes you want to add storage without adding compute and vice versa to save money. If you want to decorrelate the storage and compute, you should go to the disaggregated model.

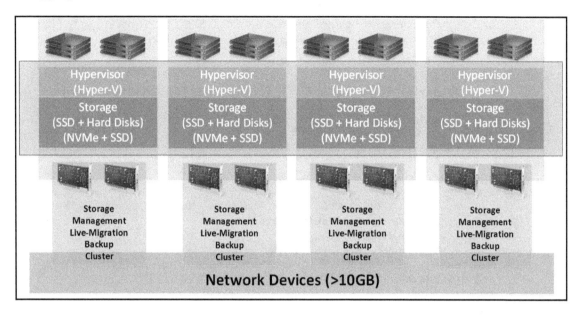

Hyperconverged model

As you can see, Hyper-V and storage are installed in the same nodes. If you have a fast network, more than 10 GB/s, you can converge all networks (we will discuss network convergence in `Chapter 5`, *Network Best Practices*).

The storage devices located in each node are aggregated in a storage pool. This is possible, thanks to the Storage Spaces Direct feature.

Each node acts as a hypervisor and a storage node. So, be careful about the CPUs and the memory for each node. Microsoft recommends at least a dual-socket server with Intel Xeon E5 family v3 or v4 with a minimum of 128 GB of memory.

This solution is very simple to deploy:

1. Spend a lot of time in the design of the solution. Choose storage and network devices, servers and architecture carefully.
2. Configure the operating system and the network. Flash all firmware to the latest version. (BIOS, storage devices, network controllers, and so on).
3. Install the required features on the nodes:

```
    Install-WindowsFeature Hyper-V, FS-FileServer, Failover-Clustering,
Data-
    Center-Bridging, RSAT-Clustering-Mgmt, RSAT-Clustering-Powershell,
RSAT-Hyper-
    V-Tools -Restart
```

4. Implement the cluster:

```
    Test-Cluster HV01, HV02, HV03, HV04 -Include "Storage Spaces Direct",
    Inventory,Network,"System Configuration"
    New-Cluster -Name HVCluster`
        -Node HV01, HV02, HV03, HV04`
        -NoStorage`
        -StaticAddress 10.10.0.164
```

5. Set the Cluster Quorum:

```
    Set-ClusterQuorum -CloudWitness`
        -Cluster FSCluster`
        -AccountName MyAzureAccount`
        -AccessKey <AccessKey>
```

6. Rename the networks:

```
    (Get-ClusterNetwork -Cluster HVCluster -Name "Cluster Network
    1").Name="Management"
    (Get-ClusterNetwork -Cluster HVCluster -Name "Cluster Network
    2").Name="Storage"
    (Get-ClusterNetwork -Cluster HVCluster -Name "Cluster Network
    3").Name="Cluster"
    (Get-ClusterNetwork -Cluster HVCluster -Name "Cluster Network
    4").Name="LiveMigration"
```

7. Configure the storage as follows:
8. Enable Storage Spaces Direct:

```
    $cluster = New-CimSession -ComputerName FSCluster
    Enable-ClusterS2D -CimSession $cluster
```

9. Create the cluster shared volume:

```
New-Volume -StoragePoolFriendlyName S2D* `
          -FriendlyName VMStorage `
          -NumberOfColumns 2 `
          -PhysicalDiskRedundancy 1 `
          -FileSystem CSVFS_REFS `
          -Size 50GB
```

At this point, you have a cluster shared volume ready to store the virtual machines. This solution is easier to deploy than the disaggregated model because you don't need the SOFS cluster role.

Storage devices configuration

Multiple mixes of storage devices are supported by Microsoft to implement Storage Spaces Direct. You can mix NVMe SSD with SATA SSD or SATA SSD with SATA HDD and even mix NVMe SSD with SATA SSD and SATA HDD (we will discuss about this special configuration in the *Multi-Resilient virtual disks* section).

Storage Spaces Direct needs performance and capacity storage devices. The most preferred performance devices, for example SSD over HDD, will be set as caching devices. The others will be used for capacity and to store virtual machines. Microsoft supports the following configurations. Depending on the storage configuration, the caching behavior changes. This is because HDD devices need a read caching while SSD are fast enough and need only write caching. The specific case of three device storage configuration will be discussed in the next section. The following table introduces each supported storage configuration in Storage Spaces Direct and the related caching behavior:

Storage Configuration	Caching devices	Capacity devices	Caching behavior
SATA SSD + SATA HDD	All SATA SSD	All SATA HDD	Read + Write
NVMe SSD + SATA HDD	All NVMe SSD	All SATA HDD	Read + Write
NVMe SSD + SATA SSD	All NVMe SSD	All SATA SSD	Write only
NVMe SSD + SATA SSD + SATA HDD (4 nodes required)	All NVMe SSD	All SATA SSD All SATA HDD	Read for SATA SSD Read + Write for SATA HDD

The capacity devices are associated with the caching devices in the round-robin manner. If a caching device fails, the others are bound to capacity devices automatically. Because of the use of the round-robin algorithm, Microsoft also recommends that the number of capacity devices should be a multiple of the number of caching devices (for example, two caching devices for 10 capacity devices). Microsoft recommends installing at least two caching devices and four capacity devices in each server.

Multi-Resilient virtual disks

From four nodes in the Storage Spaces Direct cluster, you are able to create a Multi-Resilient virtual disk. This means that you implement the caching tier with NVMe devices and the capacity tier with SSD and HDD devices. The capacity tier can be composed of a mix of storage devices type because Microsoft brings the Multi-Resilient virtual disks.

Thanks to this feature, you can create a virtual disk with a mirroring tier and a parity tier. The mirroring tier is hosted by SSD and the parity tier is hosted by HDD. Thanks to the ReFS, the data will be always written in the mirroring tier. When the mirroring tier is full, the ReFS rotates the data which is less frequently used (called also **cold data**) from the mirroring tier to the capacity tier. If a data located in the capacity tier must be updated, the ReFS invalidates the data in the capacity tier and writes a new one in the mirroring tier. This ReFS capability is called **ReFS real-time tiering**.

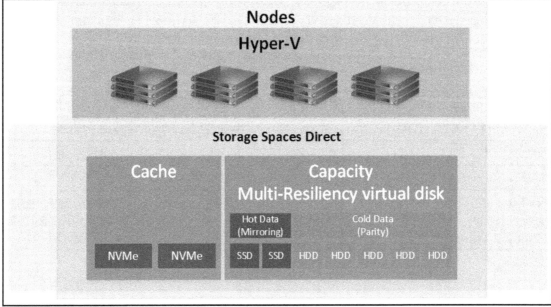

A 3-tiers storage spaces Configuration

Thanks to this feature, you can optimize performance because the data is always written in the mirroring tier with fast devices such as SSD. On the other hand, you maximize the storage capacity by using HDD in a parity resiliency. If you implement a four-nodes cluster and you need high-end performance, I recommend this kind of solution.

To create Multi-Resilient virtual disks in an existing storage pool, you have to follow these steps:

1. Create the tier in the storage pool:

```
New-StorageTier -StoragePoolFriendlyName S2D* -
FriendlyName "ColdTier" -
MediaType HDD
New-StorageTier -StoragePoolFriendlyName S2D* -
FriendlyName "HotTier" -
MediaType SSD
```

2. Create the volume:

```
New-Volume -StoragePoolFriendlyName S2D*
    -FriendlyName VMStorage02
    -FileSystem CSVFS_REFS
    -StorageTierFriendlyName HotTier, ColdTier
    -StorageTierSizes 100GB, 900GB
```

Working with virtual disks

There are several configuration options for virtual hard disks, starting from the disks format. Hyper-V supports, currently, the classic VHD format and the newer VHDX format. VHDX disks are preferable in many ways, starting with their increased size, up to 64 TB, over their better performance and reliability options, and to their better management capabilities such as resizing the disks both ways. The only reason to use VHD files now is their backwards compatibility with Hyper-V versions prior to 2012. If you don't need this, don't use VHD files. If you are still using VHD files, convert them via PowerShell when in the offline state:

```
Convert-VHD -Path d:\VM01.vhd
-DestinationPath d:\VM01.vhdx
```

After setting the format of the virtual disk, the next decision will be about the type of the virtual disk. Hyper-V supports three types of virtual hard disks:

- Fixed
- Dynamic
- Differencing

Fixed disks allocate their maximum storage at creation time. The size of a fixed disk stays the same all the time. Since all available storage is allocated at creation time, a fixed disk offers reliable and great performance.

Dynamic disks are created with just their header information and allocate more space when there is more data written to the disks. Due to their constant growth, the constant reclaiming of more storage, and editing the metadata of the virtual disk, dynamic disks have a slight performance penalty over fixed disks. The recommendation in the past for production environments with Hyper-V clearly pointed to fixed disks. However, in the current version of Hyper-V, there are great improvements in this sector too. A dynamic disk is still slower than a fixed disk, but the difference is much smaller today. There is a measurable performance hit of about 3 to 5 percent over a fixed disk in real-life scenarios. These little performance hits are not worth the management and cost downside of using fixed disks in most customer situations. In my opinion, dynamic disks should be the default option for your workload, including production systems, unless the support requirements of your application demand otherwise. Keep in mind that Hyper-V supports thin provisioning of storage; combining this with dynamic disks allows you to have a very flexible management approach for Hyper-V disks.

Differencing disks use a parent/child-relation-based linked-disk approach. A differencing disk is created and linked to a parent disk, typically containing a generalized sysprep image. A VM based on the child disk will then write all subsequent changes and customization like the child disk. These deployment scenarios are very fast and they are a great option for lab environments and VDI deployments. Differencing disks come with a high performance impact and a higher management complexity; therefore, they should not be used on production server deployments.

You can convert the disk type through PowerShell, even while converting the disk format as well:

```
Convert-VHD -Path d:\VM01.vhd`
    -DestinationPath d:\VM01.vhdx `
    -VHDType dynamic
```

There is a fourth disk type available in Hyper-V, a pass-through disk. Pass-through disks (raw) are not virtual hard disks. They directly use a physical volume without a virtualization container in between. In the past, this was a great way of achieving performance. In the recent Hyper-V versions, pass-through disks have not offered advantages but several disadvantages such as limited mobility and manageability. Therefore, do not use pass-through disks anymore. Convert them by executing the following command:

```
New-VHD -Path "D:\VMS\Converted.VHDX"
     -Dynamic -SourceDisk 5
```

On the Hyper-V host where the source disk adds the disk number from the host to convert, note that the source disk must be offline for this operation.

Cluster shared volumes

The most common question on cluster shared volumes is how many CSVs you need and how huge they may get when filled with data. As mentioned before, it's a good rule of thumb to create one CSV per cluster node; in larger environments with more than eight cluster nodes, a CSV per two to four nodes. The number of VMs per-CSV is not limited. Commonly, I do not see more than 50 VMs on a CSV for server VMs and 100 VMs for client VMs in the VDI environment. However, don't think in units here, plan in IOPS. Spread the IOPS evenly between your CSVs. To utilize the redundant storage hardware I wrote about earlier, never use a single CSV. Start with at least two CSVs to spread the load over your two storage controllers. This isn't necessarily a design of CSVs, rather a behavior of the SAN and how it manages its disks. If you use one CSV, it's possible that the SAN allocates ownership of that LUN to a single controller and could introduce a bottleneck in performance. Dividing the storage may allow the SAN to leverage an active-active configuration and potentially increase performance.

Metadata changes can only occur on the CSV coordinator, so make sure you use the CSV coordinator when applying changes such as expanding disks or moving files to the CSV. To identify the CSV coordinator, use the following cmdlet:

```
Get-ClusterSharedVolume
```

Also, identify the coordinator in the Node column. This cmdlet is also used to manage all relevant settings around CSVs. The coordinator is also known as the owner node in the Failover Cluster Manager console.

CSVs can be renamed on the filesystem level (`http://bit.ly/11A6nS7`), as well as on the cluster object level (`http://bit.ly/1vxAUFF`). This should be done prior to running any VMs from the CSV:

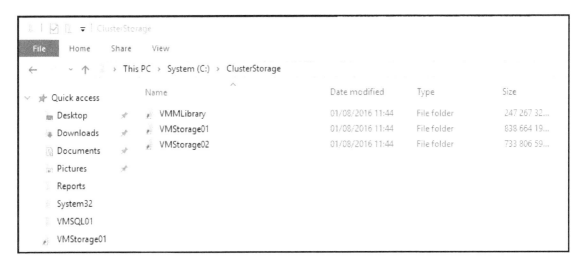

CSV renamed in file system perspective

For optimal performance on CSVs, make sure that you defrag your virtual hard disks before moving them to a CSV by adding disk images to a VM, creating checkpoints and also the VM memory itself uses space on your CSVs. When a VM is powered on, it creates a file of size equal to the RAM in the VM folder on the CSV when the automatic stop action of the VM is on save. Plan to fill up your CSVs with a maximum of 75 percent of their capacity to allow growth of all these files. If you want to know how much free space is available on your CSVs, considering all dependencies, there is a great PowerShell script available at `http://bit.ly/1mloKQC`.

Cluster shared volumes can be encrypted with Bitlocker; they will receive a performance hit around 20-30 percent. Encrypting your CSVs with Bitlocker not only increases the physical security of the data, it is also a great way to reduce the risk of data loss in case of a hard disk change for whatever reason.

CSVs comes with special configuration considerations. Make sure the network adapters used for CSVs have the client for Microsoft networks and file and printer sharing for Microsoft networks is enabled. In most cases, it's suggested that you activate Microsoft Failover Cluster Virtual Adapter Performance Filter too. However, if you are using guest cluster in your virtual machine, this setting should be disabled on the host level to avoid problems with backups and cluster options.

Enabling the CSV cache provides caching at the block level for read-only, unbuffered I/O operations by allocating system memory (RAM) as cache. 80 percent of the physical RAM can be used as a CSV cache. It's a best practice to use the CSV cache on Hyper-V Clusters. I've seen best performance/price ratios around 512-1024 MB; however, it should not be larger than 2 GB. Use the following command to configure the CSV cache in an elevated prompt to set the cache to 512 MB of data and use this value as a default for your CSV files:

```
(Get-Cluster).BlockCacheSize = 512
```

Checkpoints

Before Windows Server 2016, only standard checkpoint was available. This kind of checkpoint was not supported for all guest workloads such as Active Directory. This is why standard checkpoint was not recommended for production and was intended for use in development and test scenarios. Standard checkpoint uses save state technology to capture the hardware configuration, the data, and the state.

Microsoft has released, in Windows Server 2016, the production checkpoint, which is based on VSS for Windows guest OS and file system buffers for Linux guest OS. All production workloads are supported and this is the way to go in Windows Server 2016 in your production.

In Windows Server 2016, the production checkpoint is the default option. You can change this in the VM settings if you don't want to leverage production checkpoint:

Checkpoint configuration

Checkpoints are a great way to create points in the time of your VMs. Test updates and migrations with live exports or checkpoints of your VMs. Every time you create a checkpoint, a differencing disk will be created (AVHDX file). All changes occurring to this VM will be written to the new child disk. If you apply the checkpoint and jump back in time with your VM, the child disk will simply be deleted. If you delete the checkpoint, the two disks are merged into a clean VHDX file. Since checkpoints use differencing disks, keep in mind that every checkpoint reduces the virtual machine's performance slightly.

Besides the performance, checkpoints are hard to manage, and some tools and backup programs have issues with existing checkpoints. Checkpoints offer great flexibility; however, use them only if you really need to and delete them when you don't need them anymore.

Use the following command to create checkpoints:

```
Checkpoint-VM
    -Name Test
    -SnapshotName Snapshot1
```

There are some common best practices around checkpoints: which are as follows:

- The most important rule for checkpoints-use them as rarely as possible.
- Do not forget that checkpoints are no substitution for backups.
- Delete checkpoints as soon as possible. You can create 50 checkpoints per VM at maximum. Checkpoints impact the performance of the VM. The more checkpoints you have, the more VM performance will be degraded.
- Never delete a checkpoint file on the file level, but only through Hyper-V.
- Use standard checkpoint with caution on domain controllers and other database servers. They have prerequirements stated in their system requirements.

Data deduplication

Windows Server 2016 with Hyper-V offers built-in deduplication at no extra charge. It's a great way to reduce your storage capacity footprint with very little configuration. However, data deduplication still comes at a price-it requires additional I/O capacity. Therefore, on a general use file server, it will not affect hot data until it's reached a certain file change age. Besides the I/O-hit, volumes with active deduplication will fragment more easily causing single file operations to take longer on deduped volumes. Hyper-V takes some precautions to avoid a big performance hit, that is, every block referenced more than 100 times will be written a second time.

Real-life experiences tell us that the overall gain in saved space outweighs the performance cost on file servers, library servers, and VDI Hyper-V hosts. Running Windows data deduplication on running VMs with server workloads is not supported. Before using deduplication, you can test how much space saving dedup will get you on a volume with the PowerShell command after the dedup feature is enabled:

```
ddpeval.exe <Path>
```

Enable the dedup feature by running the following cmdlet on the host level:

```
Install-windowsFeature FS-Data-Deduplication
```

Before using deduplication, you can test how much space saving dedup will get you on a volume with the following command after the dedup feature is enabled:

```
Enable-DeDupVolume D:
```

Configure the file age needed for deduplication to occur. This directly affects the necessary storage-IOPS.

```
Set-DedupVolume -Volume D: -MinimumFileAgeDays 5
```

Start a dedup job on a specified volume:

```
Start-DedupJob D: -Type Optimization
```

To create a regular dedup schedule that will deduplicate the drive in a 10 hour window per week, use the following command:

```
New-dedupschedule -Name "Dedup01" -Type Optimization -Days Sat, Wed -
Start 23:00 -DurationHours 10
```

Keep in mind that data deduplication is not supported on system and boot volumes. That's another reason why it's a good idea to move your data to a second volume. The volume must be local, as data deduplication is not possible on removable or mapped drives.

If you already have deduplication enabled on your storage platform beneath Hyper-V, leave it there. It's more efficient to run this on the hardware/storage level. There is also a small additional storage saving by running dedup on the hardware and software levels simultaneously. However, the downsides, such as more resource utilization, overweigh, so activate dedup only on one level.

If you are using a virtual desktop infrastructure running on Hyper-V, you have hit the unique condition where it's supported to deduplicate live data. To enable deduplication of your running client VMs to ensure huge data savings, run the following command:

```
Enable-DedupVolume C:\ClusterStorage\Volume1 -UsageType HyperV
```

Keep in mind that data deduplication is a postprocessing job, so be sure there is enough storage capacity available for new data until it gets shrunk by dedup.

Storage quality of service

Microsoft has enhanced the **Storage Quality of Service** (**Storage QoS**) in Windows Server 2016. In Windows Server 2012 R2, the storage QoS policy was applied per VHDX. The Storage QoS was not agnostic to the underlying storage solution. This solution was great for a single Hyper-V, but when you have dozens of Hyper-V nodes in the cluster talking to same storage system, it doesn't work great because each Hyper-V node is not aware that they are using the same storage bandwidth.

Thanks to the enhancement of the Storage QoS (called **Distributed Storage QoS**), the policies are now stored in the cluster database. You are now able to create policies to set a minimum and/or a maximum IOPS and apply these rules to a single or multiple virtual machine/virtual hard disk. Thanks to this enhancement, the Hyper-V in a cluster using the same storage system can respect the storage QoS policies.

Distributed Storage QoS enables you to create several service levels such as a high-end performance policy (called **Gold** for example) and another with less performance. Then you can apply these policies to ensure performance for each service level.

Distributed Storage QoS in Windows Server 2016 supports only the following both scenarios:

- A storage solution based on Scale-Out File Server cluster
- A storage solution based on Hyper-V using Cluster-Shared Volume such as the hyperconverged model

Even if you are not in a multitenant environment, you should consider this feature. Some I/O intensive service such as SQL Server requires a minimum IOPS to operate in good conditions compared to a file server. With distributed Storage QoS, you can ensure that your SQL server has always the minimum IOPS required.

To implement a Distributed Storage QoS, you have to create the policy and apply it to a VHDX:

```
$CimSession = New-CimSession -ComputerName Cluster-HyperV
New-StorageQosPolicy -Name bronze -MinimumIops 50 -MaximumIops 150 -
CimSession
$CimSession
Get-VM -Name VM01 -ComputerName Cluster-HyperV |
Get-VMHardDiskDrive |
Set-VMHardDiskDrive -QoSPolicyID (Get-StorageQosPolicy -Name Bronze -
CimSession $CimSession).PolicyId
```

Here is the output:

```
PS C:\Windows\system32> Get-StorageQoSFlow -InitiatorName VM01 -CimSession $CimSession | format-list

BandwidthLimit          : 0
FilePath                : C:\ClusterStorage\Volume1\VM01\OPERATINGSYSTEM-W2016TP4.VHDX
FlowId                  : 78d2ac63-4fad-5a58-822a-078f373ffa2c
InitiatorBandwidth      : 2479104
InitiatorId             : 41aaf3ed-10bf-4eb3-b7af-fda828c34079
InitiatorIOPS           : 325
InitiatorLatency        : 13.9349
InitiatorName           : VM01
InitiatorNodeName       : HC-Nano02.int.HomeCloud.net
Interval                : 300000
Limit                   : 150
PolicyId                : ccbe3c6d-76a5-4de0-b5a2-cc6dd86b7105
Reservation             : 50
Status                  : 0k
StorageNodeBandwidth    : 2418688
StorageNodeIOPS         : 316
StorageNodeLatency      : 12.6056
StorageNodeName         : HC-Nano02.int.HomeCloud.net
TimeStamp               : 1/6/2016 3:01:07 PM
VolumeId                : 9ae24c3b-6942-48f5-bdc7-5b96a3cea323
PSComputerName          : HC-Nano01
MaximumIops             : 150
MinimumIops             : 50
```

Distributed Storage QoS applied to a VHDX

Multipath I/O

When working with highly available SAN storage systems, you not only want the storage systems to avoid a single point of failure but also its connections. Therefore, it's a best practice to have multiple connections between your SAN storage infrastructure and your Hyper-V Server systems. Multipath I/O ensures that redundant paths between these systems are detected and the corresponding disks are only registered once.

This is essential to ensure seamless disk management. With active MPIO, a path to your SAN storage might get lost without any interruption to your virtual machines. SMB3 handles this by using SMB multichannel, for all other storage architectures follow these steps to enable MPIO via PowerShell:

```
Enable-WindowsOptionalFeature -Online -FeatureName MultiPathIO
```

- If you use iSCSI Storage, run the following command:

```
Enable-MSDSMAutomaticClaim -BusType iSCSI
```

- If you use SAS storage, run the following command:

```
Enable-MSDSMAutomaticClaim -BusType SAS
```

- To ensure a round-robin switching between the available paths, run the following command:

```
Set-MSDSMGlobalDefaultLoadBalancePolicy -Policy RR
```

- It's a best practice to set the disk time-out to 60 seconds as shown in the following command:

```
Set-MPIOSetting -NewDiskTimeout 60
```

These settings are valid for the default MPIO module of Windows Server 2016 and provide optimal performance. If you are using vendor-specific storage DSMs, make sure that you consult their documentation for optimal configuration. If you have storage DSMs supported by Hyper-V available from your storage vendor, you should prefer them over the default ones.

The iSCSI target

Microsoft Windows Server includes an iSCSI target to provide iSCSI LUNs from Windows Server software instead of an iSCSI SAN. This enables you to provide central storage with whatever storage is attached to the server running the iSCSI target. The iSCSI target is supported for production. However, though there is a performance penalty against native iSCSI SAN systems, they are preferred for lab and demonstration purposes.

An iSCSI target should run on a dedicated machine and never on a Hyper-V host or another production workload-hosting server. Use PowerShell to create and configure an iSCSI target. Activate the necessary features using the following commands:

```
Add-WindowsFeature -Name FS-iSCSITarget-Server
Add-WindowsFeature -Name iSCSITarget-VSS-VDS
```

Create a new LUN:

```
New-IscsiVirtualDisk -Path d:\VHD\LUN1.vhdx -Size 60GB
```

Create a new iSCSI target:

```
New-IscsiServerTarget -TargetName Target1 -InitiatorId
IPAddress:192.168.1.240,IPAddress:192.168.1.241
```

Assign the iSCSI LUN to its target:

```
Add-IscsiVirtualDiskTargetMapping -TargetName target1 Path
d:\VHD\LUN1.vhdx -
Lun 10
```

Connect to your iSCSI target through the iSCSI initiator on your Hyper-V hosts:

```
Connect-IscsiTarget -NodeAddress <targetIQN>
```

You have the option to connect to the target from within the VMs and not from the Hyper-V hosts. This option comes with a slightly negative performance impact and additional points of administration for your storage infrastructure.

Summary

Having completed this chapter, you are now aware of the most common storage architectures for Hyper-V. You learned about the technologies used behind it and their best practice configurations.

Now, continue to `Chapter 5`, *Network Best Practices*, to learn about networking. If you want to learn even more about storage, there are some additional tuning tips in `Chapter 7`, *Hyper-V Performance Tuning*.

5

Network Best Practices

"In networking assumptions can be deadly, so while you may trust your designs, you absolutely need to verify them, learn their behavior under normal operating conditions and during failover to make sure the solutions works as designed."

Didiervan Hoye – MVP Hyper-V

This chapter will make you familiar with the common network architectures compatible with Hyper-V and show you how to use them more efficiently. A complete network virtualization solution was introduced by Windows Server 2012, which offers a huge variety of networking options for Hyper-V.

Software-defined networking (SDN) allows you to design your network independently from the physical network topology. With Windows Server 2016, a lot of new SDN features have been added and, in this chapter, we will discuss those features which are related to Hyper-V.

In this chapter, you will learn about the following topics:

- Virtual switches, vNICS, and tNICS
- NIC Teaming
- Switch Embedded Teaming
- Creating virtual networks
- Software-defined networking
- Network Controller
- IP address management (IPAM)

Networking overview

Hyper-V Network virtualization provides an abstraction layer above your physical network, quite similarly to how server virtualization provides VMs from a physical host. Network virtualization decouples virtual networks from the physical network infrastructure and removes the constraints of physical adapters, VLAN, and segregated networks on a physical level. Hyper-V Network virtualization is a big prerequisite for real flexibility in an IT infrastructure. An elastic IT infrastructure, commonly named **Cloud**, benefits from this feature and allows efficient management of networking.

In the past, the necessary multi-tenant isolation while fulfilling all security requirements could only be achieved through huge investments in network infrastructure. However, Windows Server 2016 with Hyper-V changed this. Its dynamic and flexible network approach allows you to achieve this target with less physical networking hardware but with increased flexibility. The abstraction is reached using the Hyper-V virtual switch, which is explained in the following paragraphs. Virtual machines use **virtual network interfaces** (**VIF**) that communicate through a VMBUS to the virtual switch. This complete stack is controlled by the Hyper-V root partition, also called **management OS** and the vNICs of the virtual machines.

All network-related settings in this chapter will be configured via *PowerShell* directly at the operating system level. This configuration can also be achieved through **System Center Virtual Machine Manager** (**SCVMM**), about which you will learn more in `Chapter 7`, *Hyper-V Performance Tuning*. As a rule of thumb, if you are planning to use more than three Hyper-V Hosts, the use of SCVMM is recommended and the network configuration should originate from SCVMM. It is not possible to manage network settings that were created by Hyper-V PowerShell via SCVMM.

Similar to Windows Server 2012 (R2), Windows Server 2016 supports converged networking, where different types of network traffic share the same Ethernet network infrastructure. With features such as **Quality of Service** (**QoS**), we are enabled to consolidate network traffic on fewer physical adapters. Combined with traffic isolation methods such as VLANs, you can isolate and control the network traffic completely independent of the physical design.

Let's go into the details of Hyper-V network's best practices.

Virtual switch

The Hyper-V Virtual Switch is a software-based layer-2 network switch that is available in Hyper-V Manager when you add the Hyper-V Server role. This switch allows us to connect virtual machines to both virtual networks and the physical network. In addition, the Hyper-V Virtual Switch provides policy enforcement for security, isolation, and service levels, and can be extended for advanced management purposes such as anti-virus or diagnostic additions.

You can even extend the default Hyper-V Switch with the well-known **Cisco Switch Nexus 1000V**. If you are already using Cisco Network infrastructure, you should use this extension and manage the Cisco Nexus 1000V with your existing Cisco Management infrastructure.

 There is a free version of this switch extension with essential networking features available at `http://bit.ly/1mYS9jW`. The advanced edition adds only security features known from the Nexus switching series.

Little known fact There is a free version of this switch extension with essential networking features available at http://bit.ly/1mYS9jW. The advanced edition adds only security features known from the Nexus switching series. There are three types of Hyper-V Virtual Switches available in Hyper-V. It's important to know in which situation each type is best used.

External vSwitch

The external vSwitch is bound to a physical network card in your Hyper-V host or on its abstraction layers, such as a logical teaming interface. VMs connected to this switch are able to communicate with network devices outside the Hyper-V hosts, that is, clients accessing VMs.

In `Chapter 1`, *Accelerating Hyper-V Deployment*, we already used PowerShell to create an external vSwitch:

```
New-VMSwitch -Name external -NetAdapterName "Local Area Connection 2"
```

For internal and private vSwitches, which I am going to introduce, the `NetAdapterName` parameter isn't available, since no external adapter is used. You also used the `AllowManagementOS $true` parameter earlier, which allows the same physical network adapter to be used for a virtual switch as well as for connecting to your Hyper-V hosts. This shared setup should only be used when you do not have enough physical adapters available and are not using **converged networking**, a concept I will introduce later in this chapter. Otherwise this is not a preferred configuration from a performance point of view.

Internal vSwitch

The internal vSwitch is used for communication between virtual machines on the same host as well as communication to the Hyper-V host itself. It does not allow for external communication. This is used for isolated lab environments that involve the Hyper-V host, for example, accessing different VMs from the Hyper-V host.

To create an internal vSwitch, use the following cmdlet run from an elevated shell:

```
New-VMSwitch -Name internal `
             -SwitchType internal `
             -Notes 'Internal VMs only'
```

Private vSwitch

The private vSwitch allows for communication between Hyper-V virtual machines on the same host. It does not allow for external communication or communication with the host itself. This is mainly used for guest cluster networking as described in `Chapter 2`, *Deploying Highly Available Hyper-V Clusters*, as well as for lab purposes.

To create a private vSwitch, use the following cmdlet run from an elevated shell:

```
New-VMSwitch -Name private -SwitchType Private
```

Hyper-V networking is capable of using VLANs; however, they are not configured on a vSwitch level, but on a virtual interface level. The **VLAN ID** checkbox in the Virtual Switch Manager is only intended for setting a host OS VLAN when using the `AllowManagementOS` parameter.

Virtual interface

Hyper-V offers two types of network adapters: the **legacy network adapter** and the default **synthetic network adapter**. The legacy adapter was primarily used for PXE boot capabilities. However, with only 100 MB of network bandwidth, it should be avoided. On generation 2 VMs, the legacy network adapter is no longer available and a PXE Boot is possible with the default network adapter there.

A network adapter is always connected to a vSwitch, which was described earlier in this chapter. After connecting the vmNIC to a vSwitch, we can now add this particular NIC to a specific VLAN. All network traffic to and from this VM will go through this VLAN (tagged). Instead of adding 15 different Ethernet cables to your Hyper-V host when using 15 different networks for your systems, it is a great option to enable VLAN trunking and communicate with just 1-2 physical NICs.

To add a single VLAN to our vNIC external via PowerShell, use the following cmdlet:

```
Set-VMNetworkAdapterVlan -VMName VM01 `
                         -VMNetworkAdapterName "External" `
                         -Access `
                         -VlanId 10
```

Little known fact
It is also possible to add VLAN ranges to a vNIC via trunking.

```
Set-VMNetworkAdapterVlan -VMName VM01 `
                         -Trunk `
                         -AllowedVlanIdList 1-100 `
                         -NativeVlanId 10
```

All the tagged traffic for VLANs 1-100 will be allowed to and from the VM. The untagged traffic will be defaulted to VLAN 10.

There are also additional capabilities for Hyper-V and VLANs, such as using VLAN isolation modes and promiscuous modes for more advanced scenarios with dedicated isolation and sharing requirements between VLANs (http://bit.ly/1mDy6GH).

It's best practice to stick to just one VLAN per NIC until you cannot fulfill your requirements with it. If you need to use trunking or other special scenarios, it is highly recommended that you use SCVMM for VLAN Management. Refer to Chapter 8, *Management with System Center and Azure*, for more details.

After enabling VLANs on our vNICs, we share a single or a few physical connections between these VLANs. To make sure our backup network is not using all the available bandwidth and impacting the production VMs, we use bandwidth management for our virtual interfaces, also known as **QoS**. QoS allows us to meet the service requirements of a service or an application by measuring the network bandwidth, detecting bandwidth limits, and prioritizing-or throttling-network traffic via policies. Hyper-V gives us the possibility to manage two QoS settings for networking:

- Minimum bandwidth
- Maximum bandwidth

These settings are provided on absolute bandwidth and are inflexible to hardware changes. It's best practice to set a minimum bandwidth, but don't restrict the maximum bandwidth. To set bandwidth limits leveraging this approach, use the following PowerShell cmdlet:

```
Set-VMNetworkAdapter -VMName VM1 -MinimumBandwidth 1000000
```

The absolute bandwidth is provided in bits per second and will be rounded to a byte. The settings will be reflected in the GUI:

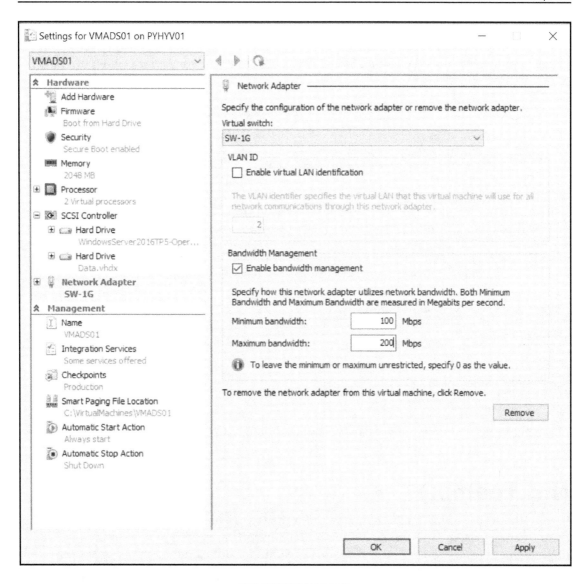

Hyper-V virtual interface properties

In this example, I've also set the maximum bandwidth to **200 Mbps**.

However, there is a far better approach using relative weights instead of absolute values. These values are not reflected in the GUI, so PowerShell is our friend again. To enable the use of weights, we first enable the vSwitch for relative weight and then set a default value to our created vSwitch.

Create a vSwitch with the `DefaultFlowMinimumBandwidthWeight` parameter as follows:

```
New-VMSwitch -Name external `
        -NetAdapterName "Local Area Connection 2" `
        -DefaultFlowMinimumBandwidthWeight
```

Set the external VMSwitch, `DefaultFlowMinimumBandwidthWeight` as `50`. This weight will be assigned to all the adapters on the vSwitch without a specific weight. Set a higher weight (up to `100`) for more important services, and less weight for less important services.

On a typical Hyper-V cluster, the following networks are available on each Hyper-V node, and I have attached my best practice bandwidth QoS configuration:

Network	QoS minimum weight
Management	10
Cluster	15
Live migration	25
Virtual machines	50

These networks and their weights are best placed on a NIC Team for redundancy.

NIC Teaming

Before Windows Server 2012, the teaming of NICs was a part of the NIC-driver but not of the operating system. This policy led to regular support cases with problematic implementations; therefore, the present NIC Teaming is done on the operating system level.

NIC Teaming in Windows Server 2016 allows us to span a team over NICs from different vendors and of different bandwidths with classic **Load Balancing and Failover** (**LBFO**) capabilities. However, it's best practice to have only active interfaces with equal bandwidth active in one team. Creating a NIC Team will create a logical network object, a **team NIC** (**tNIC**), that is then connected to our created Hyper-V vSwitch.

It's possible to create additional tNICs on an existing team without using vSwitches. However, this option lacks the ability of QoS and should be avoided.

There are different Teaming modes available in Windows Server 2012 R2. They are as follows:

- **Switch independent**: This should be your default option for newly created teams. It does not involve any configuration on involved physical switches that are connected to the teamed NICs. It's also the *must have* setting when the NICs of your team are connected to redundant switches, which are highly recommended.
- **Static Teaming**: To use static Teaming, all NICs of your team must be connected to the same switch or support **Multi-Chassis Link Aggregation**. The used switch ports must be configured for static/general Teaming.
- **LACP**: To use LACP, all the NICs of your team must be connected to the same switch or support Multi-Chassis Link Aggregation. LACP allows a semiautomatic configuration of the connected switch, preferable over static Teaming.

There are three load balancing modes available, which define how the traffic is spread among the team members. They are as follows:

- **Address hashing**: This creates hashes for outgoing network packets. Every packet with the same hash will be routed to the same network adapter. Incoming traffic is spread by the switch with switch-dependent configurations, but will use only the first NIC in the team for switch-independent configurations.
- **Hyper-V port**: This spreads the load based on the vSwitch port assignments. Single NIC-VMs will not spread their load over different network adapters, but all adapters are used for spreading all outgoing VM traffic. The same interface as the outgoing packet will be used for incoming traffic for this specific VM and not be spread over multiple adapters.
- **Dynamic**: This combines the Hyper-V port receiving the algorithm with the dynamic optimization of address hashing for outgoing packets. A sorting algorithm will optimize the hash table for more load balancing. With Windows Server 2012 R2, this leads to an effective and balanced distribution of the outbound and inbound traffic.

Let's see which combinations are ready for real-world scenarios:

- **Switch-independent configuration/Dynamic distribution**: This mode is best used for Teaming in both native and Hyper-V environments, except for guest-VM Teaming. It offers the best performance with failover capabilities.

- **Switch-independent configuration/Address hash distribution**: This mode is best used for guest-VM Teaming. Creating a team inside a VM allows the VM to be connected to more than one vSwitch. This is a typical setup in SR-IOV setups (Refer to `Chapter 7`, *Hyper-V Performance Tuning*, for details).

There is also an option to specify a standby adapter that's passive until one adapter fails. It's best practice to use all the available NICs in active teams.

Switch-dependent policies are more complex and do not provide better performance in my experience.

For more details, refer to the Windows Server 2012 R2 NIC Teaming user guide at `http://b it.ly/2b8648h`.

The main issues with NIC Teaming for Hyper-V host is the lack of support for features such as **vRSS** for NICs in management OS or RDMA. To resolve this, you can use **Switch Embedded Teaming** (**SET**) (we will discuss about SET in the next section), which is a new feature of Windows Server 2016.

With this version of Windows, I recommend that you use SET instead of NIC Teaming in the root partition. For teaming in Windows guest OS, you have to use NIC Teaming because SET is not supported in virtual machines.

Switch Embedded Teaming

When you use NIC Teaming to connect a vSwitch, you first create a teaming and then you create the vSwitch connected to the tNIC. Next, you can connect the vmNIC to the vSwitch to interconnect them. As said earlier, NIC Teaming lacks such features as vRSS for management OS or RDMA, which can be problematic for a full converged networking (we will discuss later about converged networking) and for performance.

When you use **SET**, the load balancing between NICs is managed inside the Hyper-V Switch. In a single SET, you can add a maximum of 8 physical network adapters. SET can only be used with the Hyper-V Virtual Switch in Windows Server 2016. This means that you can only deploy SET in physical nodes with the Hyper-V role installed.

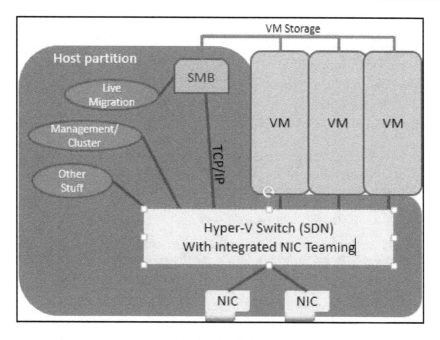

Switch embedded teaming diagram

SET supports the following features:

- Datacenter bridging (DCB)
- Hyper-V Network Virtualization: NV-GRE and VxLAN are both supported in Windows Server 2016
- Receive-side Checksum offloads (IPv4, IPv6, TCP): These are supported if any of the SET team members support them
- Remote Direct Memory Access (RDMA)
- SDN Quality of Service (QoS)
- Transmit-side Checksum offloads (IPv4, IPv6, TCP): These are supported if all of the SET team members support them
- Virtual Machine Queues (VMQ)
- Virtual Receive-side Scaling (vRSS)

However, SET doesn't support the following features:

- 802.1X authentication
- IPsec Task Offload (IPsecTO)

- QoS in host or native OSes
- Receive-side coalescing (RSC)
- Receive-side scaling (RSS)
- Single root I/O virtualization (SR-IOV)
- TCP Chimney Offload
- Virtual Machine QoS (VM-QoS)

When you use SET, the teaming mode is Switch Independent, and the load balancing algorithm can be either dynamic or Hyper-V Port. Except for an advanced scenario, I recommend that you keep the load balancing algorithm to dynamic.

To create a SET, you can run the following PowerShell cmdlet:

```
New-VMSwitch -Name SwitchSET -NetAdapterName "NIC 1","NIC 2" -
EnableEmbeddedTeaming $true -ManagementOS $True
```

When you create VMSwitch, `enableEmbeddedTeaming $True` enables the SET feature. `NetAdapterName` enables to specify the physical NIC that will be part of the SET.

If later you want to add physical NICs to the SET, you can run the following PowerShell cmdlet:

```
Set-VMSwitchTeam -Name SwitchSET -NetAdapterName "NIC 1","NIC 3"
```

The preceding cmdlet adds `NIC 1` and `NIC 3` to `SwitchSET`. If earlier `NIC 2` was in the **SwitchSET** SET, the preceding cmdlet removes it from the SET.

Converged networking

With Hyper-V Network Virtualization-VLANs, QoS, and NIC-we now have great tools at hand for creating true software-defined networking, independent of the underlying physical hardware. This enables us to implement the network design of our choice without the need for additional physical NICs. Use a few high-speed NICs instead of many single gigabit NICs. I highly recommend that you use network adapters from the same manufacturers. Even if NIC Teaming supports NICs from several vendors, I have seen a lot of issues with this kind of configuration. Team these NICs and add a converged networking solution on it. Use the virtual NICs on a vSwitch (instead of tNICs without a vSwitch) to add QoS configurations.

This offers many possibilities and there are no right or wrong options here. I'm introducing a converged network design that I have often implemented myself, and also regularly found in production environments.

A switch-independent/dynamic team is created on all available NICs of the fastest bandwidth, which are not used for guest-OS clusters. A dynamic switch is created above the team. Four vNICs will be created on the management OS and bound to the created vSwitch via PowerShell:

```
Add-VMNetworkAdapter -ManagementOS -Name "Management" -SwitchName
"External"
MinimumBandwidthWeight 10
Add-VMNetworkAdapter -ManagementOS -Name "Live Migration" -SwitchName
"External" MinimumBandwidthWeight 25
Add-VMNetworkAdapter -ManagementOS -Name "VMs" -SwitchName "External"
MinimumBandwidthWeight 50
Add-VMNetworkAdapter -ManagementOS -Name "Cluster" -SwitchName
"External"
MinimumBandwidthWeight 15
```

The result will be a very flexible networking solution fulfilling all our Hyper-V requirements for production workloads. The following screenshot shows a converged network. You can see three virtual network adapter bound to the switch called **SW-1G**:

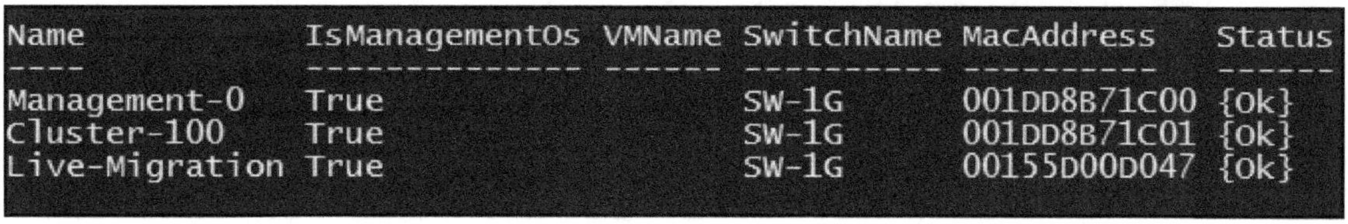

```
Name            IsManagementOs VMName SwitchName MacAddress    Status
----            -------------- ------ ---------- ----------    ------
Management-0    True                  SW-1G      001DD8B71C00  {Ok}
Cluster-100     True                  SW-1G      001DD8B71C01  {Ok}
Live-Migration  True                  SW-1G      00155D00D047  {Ok}
```

Three virtual NICs bound to the same virtual switch

It's highly recommended that you use a converged architecture instead of a classical physical mapping of networks.

Storage network

If you are using **Fibre Channel Infrastructure** for storage communication, you don't need additional considerations to integrate this communication into your converged network. However, if you are using the iSCSI communication, it's highly recommended that you use another network for storage communication. The iSCSI communication uses MPIO for resiliency instead of network teaming. There is just one upcoming scenario where iSCSI over teamed interfaces is possible, in all the major scenarios teaming iSCSI communication is not supported. Refer to `http://bit.ly/1mVYDyq` for more details.

It's best practice to separate the iSCSI communication from other traffic on a host level, so use two dedicated network cards on the host. Don't add them to a team, instead use the MPIO feature for resiliency.

If you are using SMB3 communication for your storage, use Switch Embedded Teaming to converge this kind of traffic if your network adapters support RDMA. To give the priority to SMB3 flow over the others on networks, you can leverage (**DCB**Datacenter Bridging (DCB) and **Priority Flow Control** (**PFC**). To install and configure DCB for SMB3, run the following script:

```
# Turn on DCB
Install-WindowsFeature Data-Center-Bridging
# Set a policy for SMB-Direct
New-NetQosPolicy "SMB" -NetDirectPortMatchCondition 445 -
PriorityValue8021Action 3
# Turn on Flow Control for SMB
Enable-NetQosFlowControl  -Priority 3
# Make sure flow control is off for other traffic
Disable-NetQosFlowControl  -Priority 0,1,2,4,5,6,7
# Apply policy to the target adapters
Enable-NetAdapterQos  -InterfaceAlias "SLOT 2*"
# Give SMB Direct 30% of the bandwidth minimum
New-NetQosTrafficClass "SMB"  -Priority 3  -BandwidthPercentage 30  -
Algorithm
ETS
```

To create a vNIC on a SET with RDMA capability, run the following cmdlets:

```
Add-VMNetworkAdapter -SwitchName SETswitch -Name SMB_1 -managementOS
Add-VMNetworkAdapter -SwitchName SETswitch -Name SMB_2 -managementOS
Enable-NetAdapterRDMA "vEthernet (SMB_1)","vEthernet (SMB_2)"
```

You can also create an affinity between a vNIC and a physical network adapter. This does not prevent the vNIC from failing over to another NIC if the first fails. But, if you have two vNICs connected to a SET with two physical NICs, you can bind a vNIC to a physical NIC and the second vNIC with the second physical NIC. You can make this affinity using PowerShell as follows:

```
Set-VMNetworkAdapterTeamMapping -VMNetworkAdapterName SMB_1 -
ManagementOS -
PhysicalNetAdapterName NIC 1
Set-VMNetworkAdapterTeamMapping -VMNetworkAdapterName SMB_2 -
ManagementOS -
PhysicalNetAdapterName NIC 2
```

SMB Direct

When using SMB3 storage communication or live migration, it is recommended that you install RDMA network adapters for best performance. Since Windows Server 2016, you can converge SMB traffic with other traffic using SET as seen earlier. You can add each network adapter in the same subnet, and Windows Server 2016 will automatically configure these networks in the failover cluster.

Windows Server will also automatically spread the workload between the NICs using SMB multichannel. RDMA enables high-performance networking while using very little CPU load. SMB Direct will be automatically enabled when RDMA-capable NICs are detected on the host.

There are three types of RDMA-aware network architectures available. They are as follows:

- **ROCE**: This stands for **RDMA over converged Ethernet** and utilizes existing Ethernet network switches. Since RoCEv2, it is not complex to implement and it is a routable protocol. For details and implementation guidelines, refer to `http://bit.ly/1miEA97`. This is the standard that I recommend.
- **iWARP**: This uses a connection-oriented transport instead of the link-based ROCE. It is way easier to implement and to maintain in my experience, but still, Ethernet utilizes existing Ethernet network switches. There are far less support calls per implementation from customers using iWARP over ROCE. It is a routable protocol; so, you can use it across datacenters. For details and implementation guidelines, refer to `http://bit.ly/1ebTrCc`.

- **InfiniBand**: InfiniBand uses its own network architecture and does not leverage existing Ethernet infrastructure. It offers great performance and huge bandwidths for a significant entry price. InfiniBand is your choice if you want performance without trade-offs. For details and implementation guidelines, refer to `http://bit.ly/1tTe7IK`. This last is not supported by Storage Spaces Direct.

All three types of architecture have the ability to provide a great performance for SMB storage communication and Live Migration. It is not necessary, in my experience, to use RDMA capabilities if you are not using 10 GB Ethernet or greater bandwidths for VM networking.

Advanced networking options

After configuring our converged fabric, it's now time to take a look at more advanced networking configuration options in Hyper-V. To take the level of network virtualization even further, it's possible to run virtual machines with the same IP addresses on the same network without causing conflicts.

The techniques used for this are mainly NVGRE for encapsulation and an NVGRE gateway for outside communication. These are great options, but not commonly needed. Stay away from these settings until you really need to use them. Since uncommon options are not the focus of this book, refer to `http://bit.ly/Ud5WXq` for details.

A far more common option is the use of **DHCP Guard**. Having a Roque DHCP Server on the network can very quickly become a very ugly problem for nearly every production environment. A Windows DHCP Server in an Active Directory Domain must be authorized until it starts broadcasting DHCP offers. In other topologies, nothing else stops Roque DHCP Servers. Hyper-V can protect you from unsolicited router and DHCP Server offers at a network level.

It's best practice to enable DHCP Guard for all VMs and disable it for particular VMs where these services are needed. Of course, we use PowerShell for this task as follows:

```
Get-VM | Set-VMNetworkAdapter -DhcpGuard On
```

This is not enabled by default, since there is a minimal performance impact for filtering out unsolicited DHCP packets at a network level. In my experience, this performance hit is virtually unmeasurable.

There is a similar service called **Router Guard** for filtering ICMP Router Advertisements and redirect messages, but the use of Router Guard is very uncommon.

Network controller

Microsoft has released a new feature called Network Controller with Windows Server 2016. This is a highly available and scalable service to manage Software-defined Networking from a single pane. Network Controller provides two APIs. They are as follows:

- **SouthBound API**: This API enables you to detect, gather network information, and send configuration to devices such as Hyper-V virtual switches, Software load balancer, Datacenter Firewall, and Remote Access Service.
- **Northbound API**: This API enables you to interact with Network Controller. Thanks to this API, you can monitor, troubleshoot, deploy, and configure new devices through PowerShell.

The Network Controller can be managed using PowerShell or using GUI with, for example, System Center Virtual Machine Manager.

Network Controller is beyond the scope of this book. Just remember that you can configure Hyper-V virtual switches through Network Controller.

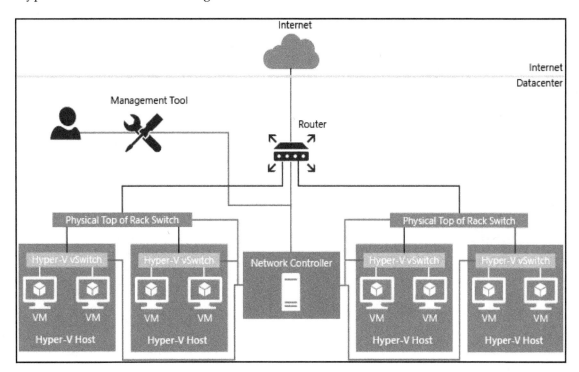

Network controller diagram

IPAM

One of my most favorite features in Windows Server 2016 is the **IP address management** (**IPAM**) module. It's very simple and quick to use, but also very effective.

When you need a static IP address for a newly created virtual machine, from where do you obtain it? Ping a random address and see whether it times out? Check the DNS server for records? Check the DHCP leases and reservations or an outdated Excel file? All of these are common processes, but there is still a chance of failure and use of those IP addresses which are already in use.

IPAM offers a dynamic version of the Excel list. It periodically scans your DNS and DHCP Servers to document all the taken IP addresses and offers the next *real free* IP address that you can use for your new VM, and have it documented automatically.

I do not know of a way to configure IPAM completely through PowerShell, so I recommend that you follow the guide available at `http://bit.ly/1qgEw1R`.

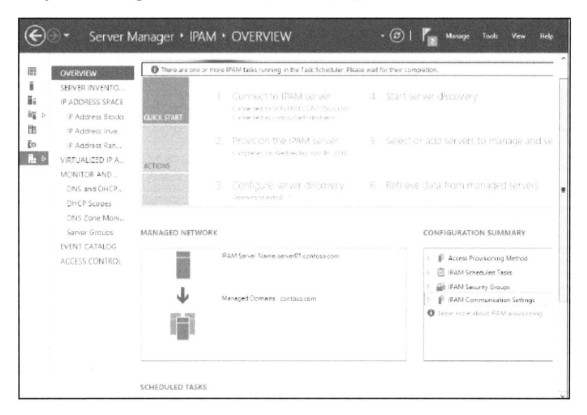

IPAM

Summary

Having completed this chapter, you should now be familiar with best practice options to configure a basic Hyper-V network, utilizing the potential of converged networking.

Now, continue to `Chapter 6`, *Highly Effective Hyper-V Design*, to learn to make a Hyper-V design with NAS, SAN, or Storage Spaces Direct.

6

Highly Effective Hyper-V Design

"Implementing Microsoft Hyper-V™ can increase security, improve business continuity, drive down costs, and deliver the business agility you need to gain a competitive edge in a rapidly changing business environment today. However, the planning and designing phase is imperative essential for a successful implementation of a Hyper-V infrastructure. Start with Microsoft Assessment and Planning (MAP) Toolkit and know your requirements. Follow the best practices discussed in this book to avoid missing any vital step during the designing phase."

Charbel Nemnom – MVP Cloud and Datacenter Management

This chapter provides some guidance to design a Hyper-V infrastructure considering your needs and estimated budget. Several designs involving iSCSI NAS, SAN, and Storage Spaces Direct storage system solution will be explained. The main goal of this chapter is to help you choose a well-known Hyper-V design to ease the deployment and the management.

This chapter includes the following topics:

- Designing a Hyper-V cluster with a NAS/SAN
- Designing a disaggregated model with Storage Spaces Direct
- Designing a hyperconverged model with Storage Spaces Direct

Cautious network selection

Network is a key component for a first-class Hyper-V infrastructure. With a bad network design, you can expect poor performance, scalability, and stability. In the project where I was involved, I've often seen network underestimated. The chosen network adapters were the cheapest available and it was unusual that the NIC features were compared with others.

Moreover, it is often the network team which determines the design without consulting the system team. For example, the network team knows LACP perfectly for network high availability and doesn't want to implement a teaming without this technology, but the recommended way of teaming in Windows Server 2016 is using dynamic algorithm.

Because of the underestimated network design, the Hyper-V performances are not always as expected. The network design depends firstly on the storage and compute design that you have chosen. For example, a solution based on iSCSI NAS should require at least two dedicated NICs for storage traffic. A hyperconverged solution requires RDMA ready NICs with 10 GB/s at least.

To begin, choose the storage and compute solution which fits your needs and your estimated budget. Then the network design should be the result of the chosen solution. To finish, consult your network team about the design and why you need this kind of solution.

Hyper-V cluster with SAN or NAS

So far, virtualization infrastructures have been built with a SAN or NAS storage system. Hyper-V is able to work with these kinds of solution using iSCSI or **Fibre Channel** (**FC**) protocol. This section introduces the Hyper-V design with both solutions.

iSCSI architecture overview

The solution presented in the following diagram is based on a NAS or a SAN and iSCSI protocol for storage traffic.

To implement this solution, the following hardware are required:

- At least two Hyper-V nodes for high availability (three or more are recommended)
    - Two NICs dedicated to iSCSI traffic
    - Two NICs dedicated to management, clustering, live migration, and VM networks

- At least two Ethernet switches. The speed of the Ethernet port must be related to the speed of the NAS or SAN Ethernet port and Hyper-V NICs. For example, if you have bought a NAS with 10 GB/s NIC, you should also buy 10 GB/s switches.

- An iSCSI SAN or NAS with two controllers to ensure high availability. In the following diagram, each controller has two Ethernet ports. The storage capacity depends on your needs. Usually, the more disks you have, the more performance you have.

This solution is the cheapest solution involving a shared hardware storage system. This is because you can use the classical Ethernet switches and Ethernet NICs in Hyper-V nodes. However, it is not the most efficient solution because of the iSCSI protocol. In the next section, we will discuss the configuration of this solution from the operating system, networking, and storage perspectives.

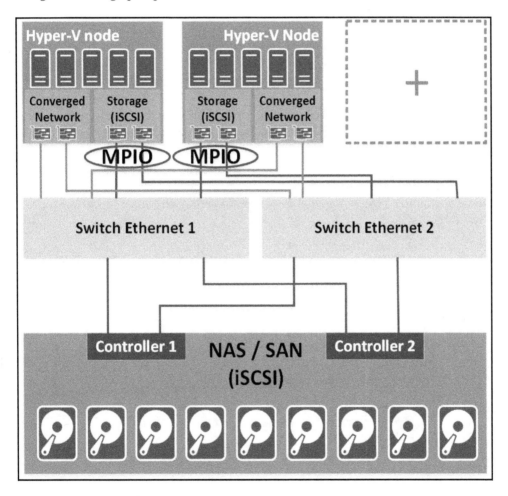

Hyper-V Cluster connected to a NAS or a SAN with iSCSI

Fibre channel architecture overview

The following solution is nearly the same as iSCSI, except that the FC protocol is used between Hyper-V nodes and the SAN. To implement this solution, you need the following hardware:

- At least two Hyper-V nodes for high availability (three are recommended, to not consume half of the resources for high availability):
    - Two **Host Bus Adapters** (**HBA**) per node which support FC
    - Two NICs dedicated for management, clustering, Live Migration, and VM networks per node
- At least two Ethernet switches. The speed of the Ethernet port must be related to the speed of Hyper-V NICs. For example, if you have bought 10 GB/s NIC, you should also buy 10 GB/s switches.
- At least two FC Switches, to interconnect SAN and Hyper-V nodes.
- Two SAN controllers, to ensure high availability. In the following diagram, each controller has FC port. The storage capacity depends on your needs. Usually, the more disks you have, the more performance you have.

This solution delivers more storage performance than iSCSI NAS/SAN because it provides high-end performance. This solution is also more expansive because of HBA, FC switches, and optical fibres.

This solution also requires the storage team to configure the zoning, the masking, the LUN, and so on.

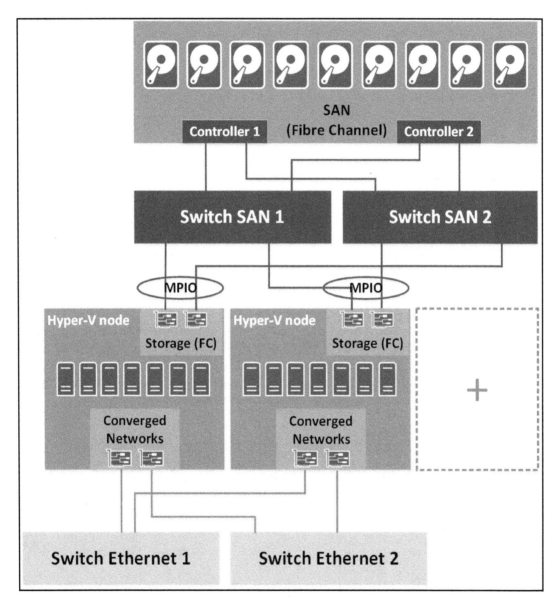

Hyper-V cluster connected to a SAN using FC protocol

Network configuration

To implement these solutions, we will leverage network convergence (discussed in `Chapter 5`, *Network Best Practices*) for management (Active Directory, remote session, administration, and so on), cluster heartbeat, live migration, and VM networks. Only the storage traffic will be handled on dedicated hardware (Ethernet NIC for iSCSI and HBA for FC). The following is an example of IP addressing plan and associated VLAN:

- **Management**: `10.10.10.0/24` (VLAN ID: 10); this should be the native VLAN
- **Cluster**: `10.10.11.0/24` (VLAN ID: 11)
- **Live migration**: `10.10.12.0/24` (VLAN ID: 12)
- (iSCSI only) **Storage 01**: `10.10.13.0/24` (VLAN ID: 13)
- (iSCSI only) **Storage 02**: `10.10.14.0/24` (VLAN ID: 14)
- **VM networks 01**: `10.10.100.0/24` (VLAN ID: 100)
- **VM networks 02**: `10.10.101.0/24` (VLAN ID: 101)

The management network should be the native VLAN to ease the deployment of Hyper-V across the network using, for example, Virtual Machine Manager. We will discuss about Virtual Machine Manager in `Chapter 8`, *Management with System Center and Azure*.

In case of iSCSI, there are two storage networks, because each server has two NICs dedicated to storage and each controller in the storage system also has two network adapters. Each server as well as each NAS/SAN controller will use one IP in both storage networks. Most of the time, jumbo frame reduces CPU cycles and increases performance when it is used for storage. Before implementing it, make sure that your switches support this feature. You should perform a test with this feature enabled to validate proper functioning with jumbo frame.

To finish, LACP or other network teaming protocols will be not configured from the switches perspectives. Instead, it is Windows Server 2016 that will manage high availability as MPIO for storage and Switch Embedded Teaming for network convergence. Each switch port will be configured to support VLAN in the access mode for the storage port and in the trunk mode for other traffics.

Storage configuration

If your SAN/NAS supports **Offloaded Data Transfer** (**ODX**), I recommend that you enable this feature to increase storage performance.

Regarding storage configuration, you should configure it to have at least two levels of performance. For example, you can create a LUN hosted in a RAID 10 and another located in a RAID 5. In this way, a highly intensive application, such as a database, can be stored in a RAID 10 and a less intensive VHDX in a RAID 5. A virtual machine composed of several VHDXs can spread its virtual hard disks across multiple LUN. For example, the operating system VHDX can be hosted in a RAID 5 while the VHDX which handles database can be hosted in a RAID 10. This avoids the consumption of all the RAID 10 storage space just for the operating system or for a low intensive application.

If a LUN must be bound to a virtual machine, avoid using pass through disks. If the LUN is intended to be shared across several VMs for guest clustering, prefer using the VHD Set (mentioned in `Chapter 2`, *Deploying Highly Available Hyper-V Clusters*). If the LUN is intended for any other usages, as backup volume for example, you can accomplish the implementation in two different ways depending on the underlying storage solution:

- **iSCSI storage**: I recommend that you create two additional virtual network adapters per VM and follow these few steps:
    - Create a virtual switch per storage physical NIC
    - For each virtual switch, create a virtual network adapter for the management OS bound to this virtual switch
    - Connect each virtual network adapter of the VM to one virtual switch
    - Configure the iSCSI initiator and MPIO in the VM
- **FC storage**: I recommend that you create two additional HBA per node with NPIV enabled and follow these few steps:
    - Create two virtual SAN (one per HBA dedicated to NPIV)
    - Create two virtual HBA for the VM (each bound to one virtual SAN)

- Make the zoning and the masking for these HBA. Be careful, two **World Wide Names** (**WWNs**) are created per virtual HBA to support the live migration of the VM

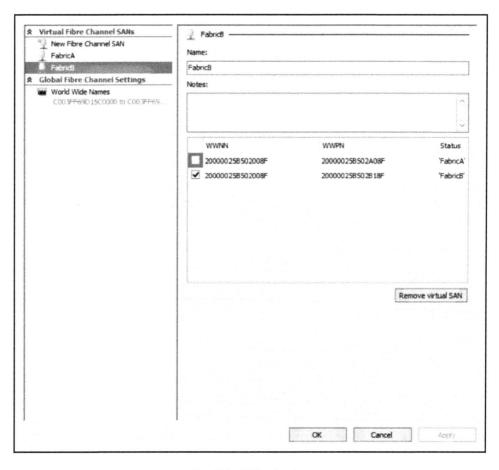

Hyper-V virtual SAN configuration

Operating system configuration

Both solutions require the same features to work with a iSCSI NAS or a FC SAN. Each node requires these features:

- Hyper-V role
- Failover Clustering feature
- MPIO feature

If you are using iSCSI NAS, don't forget to enable the service called **Microsoft iSCSI Initiator Service** in the automatic startup type to establish the connection to the NAS/SAN when the server starts.

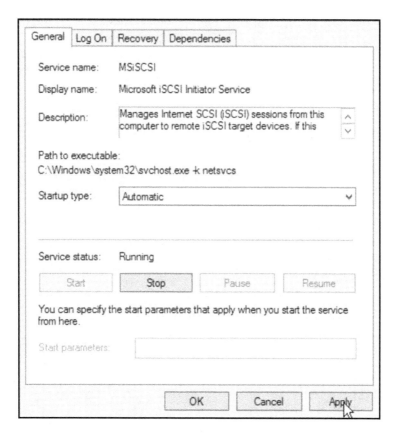

Configure the Microsoft iSCSI Initiator Service to start automatically

If you are implementing either iSCSI NAS or FC SAN, you need to deploy a Switch Embedded Teaming with the dedicated NICs. Then, create and configure virtual network adapters as discussed in Chapter 5, *Network Best Practices*, for clustering, live migration, management, and VM networks.

Once the network is configured and the nodes are reachable, you can configure the storage. The storage configuration is different depending on the underlying storage system.

iSCSI configuration

The storage system will deliver four iSCSI targets (two per controller). From the Hyper-V perspective, two iSCSI initiators exist per node. Regarding this configuration, four iSCSI paths will be created (two per storage NIC) in the iSCSI initiator.

Each NIC should be connected to each storage controller. In case a storage controller is down, two iSCSI paths will still work. In case a network adapter is down, the other also will be connected with two iSCSI paths. With this design, you ensure a high availability of the storage connection.

Once the iSCSI initiator is configured, you have to enable MPIO and add support for iSCSI devices.

MPIO configuration

If you don't enable this setting, you will see several instances of each LUN. In this example, you will see four instances of each LUN-one per iSCSI path. To spread the storage workload across all iSCSI paths, MPIO adds a storage device driver. When MPIO is enabled, just one instance of the disk is shown and all the iSCSI paths are used simultaneously to increase the bandwidth and the availability.

Before implementing the cluster, I highly recommend that you try to disconnect some devices to try the high availability of the solution.

When LUN are mounted in each Hyper-V nodes, you can implement the cluster as mentioned in Chapter 2, *Deploying Highly Available Hyper-V Clusters*.

SAN configuration

An FC SAN requires much more configuration than a iSCSI NAS/SAN. First, be sure that your HBA is up to date and that the firmware and drivers are supported by the switches and the SAN itself. The firmware and drivers between SAN, switches, and HBA must be supported for the best stability and performance. I have seen some projects where firmware is not compatible and so the solution was not really stable (LUN disconnected, performance issues, and so on).

Second, you have to configure MPIO. Each SAN vendor provides **Device-Specific Modules (DSMs)**, which properly configure MPIO to work with the storage system. This DSM should be indicated in the SAN documentation. I have seen some vendors that provide a package that install the MPIO feature and configure it. Others provide only an INF. In either way, you have to configure MPIO properly as indicated in the vendor documentation.

Third, you have to communicate the WWN of each HBA to the storage team. Then they will make the zoning and the masking. When these steps are executed and a LUN is created, you should see a LUN mounted in each Hyper-V node. If you do not see the LUN, try to refresh your storage devices in disk management.

Before implementing the cluster, I highly recommend that you disconnect some devices to try the high availability. For example, you can try to shut down a SAN controller, a switch, or an HBA. If the solution keeps working with the expected performance, you can move forward and you can implement the cluster as discussed in Chapter 2, *Deploying Highly Available Hyper-V Clusters*.

Storage Spaces Direct design

If you are looking for a more modern approach than using a hardware storage system, you will find this section interesting. Instead of using a NAS or a SAN, Storage Spaces enables you to deploy a Software-Defined Storage. In this section, two deployment models will be introduced, which leverage Storage Spaces Direct as seen in `Chapter 4`, *Storage Best Practices*. These models are called **disaggregated** and **hyperconverged**.

Network design

Before introducing each model available with Storage Spaces Direct, let's talk about network. Both solutions require the same network topology. The only difference is the location of the storage-in dedicated nodes or in the compute nodes. However, with both solutions you need the same network addressing plan. You require a management network (nodes deployment, Active Directory, remote session, administration, and so on), a live migration network, a cluster heartbeat network, a storage network, and all the VM networks. Instead of creating several storage networks, as we have done in iSCSI solution, with Microsoft Software-Defined Storage you can include all traffics in a single storage network. This is possible, thanks to the new Windows Server 2016 feature called **Simplified SMB Multichannel** (`http://bit.ly/2bCcHir`).

The following is an example of an IP network addressing plan:

- **Management**: `10.10.10.0/24` (VLAN ID: 10); this should be the native VLAN
- **Cluster**: `10.10.11.0/24` (VLAN ID: 11)
- **Live migration**: `10.10.12.0/24` (VLAN ID: 12)
- **Storage**: `10.10.13.0/24` (VLAN ID: 13)
- **VM Network 01**: `10.10.100.0/24` (VLAN ID: 100)

- **VM Network 02**: `10.10.101.0/24` (VLAN ID: 101)

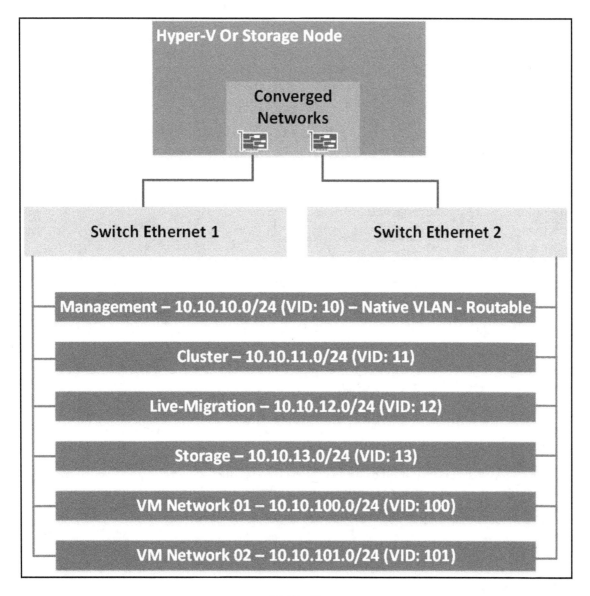

Network topology

The management network should be the native VLAN to ease the deployment of Hyper-V across the network using, for example, Virtual Machine Manager. We will discuss about Virtual Machine Manager in `Chapter 8`, *Management with System Center and Azure*.

In either the storage or compute node, SET will be implemented to be able to make a fully converged network. Some virtual network adapters in the management OS require RDMA. Moreover, we need a high speed network adapter (at least 10 GB/s), so we have to leverage vRSS in the root partition for highest performance. This is why SET is required.

To ease the implementation of a fully converged network, I recommend that you implement the **RDMA over the Converged Ethernet** (**RoCE**) solution. In the version 2 of RoCE, the traffic can now be routable.

When you have created the virtual network adapters dedicated to storage and live migration, don't forget to enable RDMA:

```
Enable-NetAdapterRdma -Name Storage01
```

Because we will leverage SET, the switches will be not configured to use LACP for network high availability. The network high availability will be handled by the operating system.

As mentioned earlier, the network is same for both the Storage Spaces Direct deployment models. Let's introduce both models to help you to choose the design which fits your needs.

Disaggregated model

The disaggregated model shown in the following diagram requires two clusters-one for compute and one for storage. This solution is based on Windows Server 2016 technologies and Ethernet for the network.

The storage cluster is composed of three nodes at least. However, a four-node cluster brings you more features, such as multi-resilient virtual disks. This cluster can be extended to 16 nodes.

From the compute perspective, you need at least two nodes; however, I recommend three nodes to not consume half of the resources for the high availability. This cluster can be extended to 64 nodes.

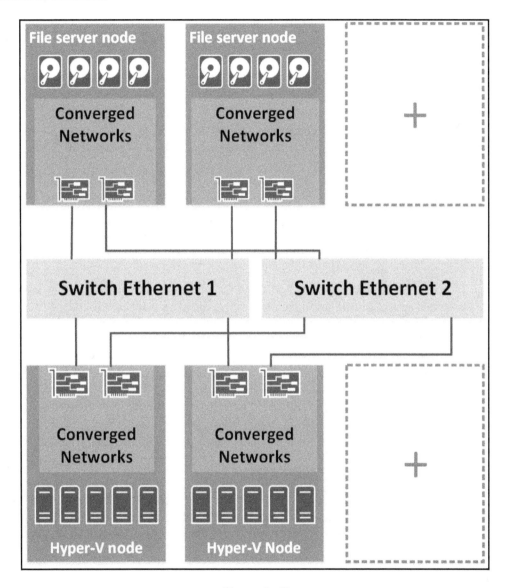

Disaggregated model

To implement this solution, you need the following hardware:

- A cluster with at least two nodes for the storage cluster (four nodes are required for some features such as multi-resilient virtual disks):
    - Each node requires two 10 GB/s NICs at least with RDMA ready. I recommend mellanox hardware with RoCEv2 (`http://bit.ly/2b pSrQu`).
    - Each node needs two cache storage devices and capacity storage devices. For more information, refer to `Chapter 4`, *Storage Best Practices*.
    - Each TB of cache requires 10 GB of memory. For example, if you plan to implement 4 TB of cache, you need at least 40 GB of memory.

- A cluster with at least two nodes for the compute cluster (I recommend three nodes):
    - Each node requires 10 GB/s NICs at least with RDMA ready. I recommend Mellanox hardware with RoCEv2 (`http://bit.ly/2b pSrQu`).
- Two Ethernet switches ready with RoCEv2, DCB, PFC, and ETS technologies. The switches speed should be in relation to the network adapters installed in servers.

Regarding licensing cost, the disaggregated model is more expensive than the hyperconverged model. You need Windows Server licenses for the storage and compute nodes. However, if you want to dissociate the storage and compute nodes, this is the solution to go with. If you know that you will add more Hyper-V nodes than storage, the hardware cost could be less than that of the hyperconverged model. Nevertheless, you need to handle the scalability of each pane.

Storage nodes configuration

In the disaggregated model, the storage configuration is made only from the storage nodes. These nodes require internal disks or disks in a SAS connected JBOD enclosure. The disks can be SAS disks, SATA disks, or NVMe disks. The faster disks will be selected for the cache mechanism.

In this model, the Hyper-V nodes access the storage using the SMB 3 protocol. To provision the SMB shares, the Scale-Out File Server feature will be deployed in the storage cluster.

To deploy the storage solution, you need to install the following features:

- Failover clustering
- Datacenter bridging
- File server role

Next, you have to create the SET as described in Chapter 5, *Network Best Practices*. Then you have to create four virtual network adapters:

- 1x for management
- 1x for cluster heartbeat
- 2x for storage usage (require RDMA)

To leverage both physical network adapters equally, you should create an affinity rule between each storage virtual network adapter dedicated to storage and a physical network adapter (for further information, refer to the SMB Direct section in Chapter 5, *Network Best Practices*). Then, don't forget to apply a QoS weight on each network adapter.

Next, configure the nodes as described in Chapter 4, *Storage Best Practices*. Don't forget to configure datacenter bridging to leave the priority to SMB traffics. Regarding the storage virtual NICs, you don't need more configuration because **Simplified SMB MultiChannel** will perform the configuration for you.

The switches must be also configured to support DCB and RDMA.

I highly recommend that you format volume using ReFS to leverage accelerated VHDX operation. This will decrease the time for some maintenance tasks such as fixed VHDX creation or merging a checkpoint. The multi-resilient virtual disk also requires ReFS.

Once Scale-Out File Server is ready and the SMB shares are created, the storage solution is ready and the compute nodes can use it to store VM.

Compute nodes configuration

There are not many configurations to execute for the compute nodes. First, you need to install the following features:

- Hyper-V role
- Datacenter bridging
- Failover clustering

Then create the SET as described in `Chapter 5`, *Network Best Practices*. You need five virtual network adapters:

- 1x for management
- 1x for cluster heartbeat
- 1x for live migration (requires RDMA)
- 2x for storage (require RDMA)

Next, configure the network as the storage node. Create the affinity rule between each storage virtual network adapter and physical network adapter and set QoS weight on each virtual network adapter. To finish, configure datacenter bridging (for further information, refer to the SMB Direct section in `Chapter 5`, *Network Best Practices*).

You can now try to access the SMB Share located in the storage node. If you can access the SMB share, you can create a VM by specifying the UNC of the share.

Hyperconverged model

The second design available when using Storage Spaces Direct is the hyperconverged model. The main difference, compared with the disaggregated model, is that storage is no longer handled by a dedicated storage node. In the hyperconverged model, the storage devices are located in the compute node. The storage devices can be connected internally or externally with a SAS connected JBOD enclosure. Disks can be SATA disks, SAS disks, or NVMe disks.

For this kind of solution, you need at least two nodes. Some features such as multi-resilient virtual disks and erasure coding are only available from four nodes. This cluster can be extended to 16 nodes.

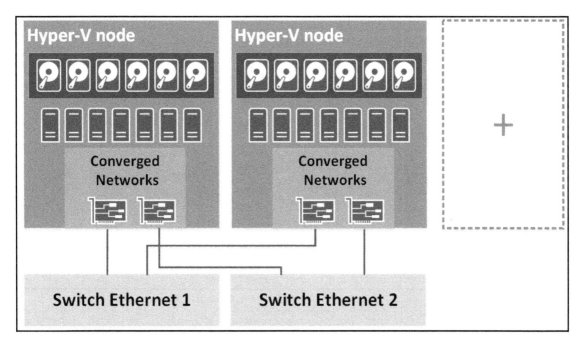

Hyperconverged model

The main advantage of this solution is the flexibility and the scalability. Each time you add a node, you simultaneously add compute and storage resources. If you use high-speed network adapters (40 GB/s for example), you can install only two NICs in each node. This means that you have only three network cables connected to each node-one for **baseboard management controller** (**BMC**) and two for network adapters. This configuration eases also the network configuration and the cabling management.

Some hardware vendors sell a four-node solution in the same 2U chassis. This is a good solution for scalability, but be careful about the number of disks per node. Usually, you can connect a limited number of disks for each node due to the small form factor. If you want to connect a larger number of disks, prefer using the classical rack servers.

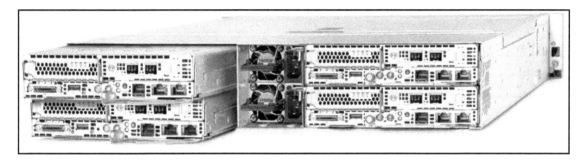

HP hyperconverged system

This solution is the cheapest from the software license perspective. You need only one Windows Server 2016 Datacenter license per node. In the disaggregated model, you need more licenses because there are more nodes deployed. If we compare with the hardware SAN system, usually you have extra licenses for the SAN itself and for the Fibre Channel Switches.

From the hardware cost perspective, this solution is more expensive than the disaggregated model in some case. For example, if you want to just add more computer resources, in the hyperconverged model you also have to buy storage resources. The hyperconverged model is usually less expensive than a hardware storage system also (compared to the same capacity and performance).

To deploy a hyperconverged solution, you need the following hardware:

- At least two nodes (I recommend at least four nodes for storage efficiency and resiliency):
    - Each node requires at least 128 GB of memory and a dual CPU with as good performance as Intel Xeon E5 family v3/v4.
    - Each node requires at least two caches storage devices and capacity storage devices.
    - Each node requires 10 GB of memory for each 1 TB of cache. Be careful about the memory consumption between compute and storage usage. For example, if you plan to implement 4 TB of cache, you need at least 40 GB of memory.

- Each node requires two 10 GB/s NICs at least with RDMA ready. I recommend Mellanox hardware with RoCEv2 (http://bit.ly/2bpSrQu).

- Two Ethernet switches ready with RoCEv2, DCB, PFC, and ETS technologies. The speed of the switches should be in relation to the network adapters installed in servers.

This solution is also easy to deploy. Each node requires these features:

- Hyper-V role
- Datacenter bridging
- Failover clustering

Once you have installed these features, you have to deploy a SET, as described in Chapter 5, *Network Best Practices*. With this solution, you need at least five virtual network adapters:

- 1x for management
- 1x for cluster heartbeat
- 1x for live migration (requires RDMA)
- 2x for storage (require RDMA)

Once you have created SET and configured each virtual network adapters, don't forget to configure DCB, as described in Chapter 5, *Network Best Practices*.

Then you can create the cluster and implement Storage Spaces Direct, as described in `Chapter 4`, *Storage Best Practices*.

Summary

With the introduction of several Hyper-V designs, you are now able to choose the right model which fits your needs and your estimated budget. Despite a good design, you may want to implement some tuning to gain the maximal performance that your infrastructure can provide. In `Chapter 7`, *Hyper-V Performance Tuning,* you will learn which performance counters are important and how to perform the tuning that increases overall performance.

Hyper-V Performance Tuning

7

"Guesswork is the path to failure. Start on a good footing with MAP and know your requirements. Follow the best practices of this book to avoid most performance issues. And practice monitoring your hosts and workloads so you can quickly fix issues if they happen."

Aidan Finn – MVP Hyper-V

After completing the basic configuration of all Hyper-V components, it's now time for additional performance tuning.

These are the topics that we will cover in this chapter:

- Measuring performance
- Performance tuning and sizing guidelines for:
    - Hardware
    - Storage/network
    - Hyper-V server role
- Benchmarking
- Tuning for client virtualization and virtual GPUs

Measuring performance

Before we start getting into performance tuning, it's necessary to have an understanding of the current situation. Many instances of sizing for Hyper-V setups, have seemingly been based on some random goodwill rough estimates without recognizing the current situation or future requirements. A far better approach to size Hyper-V setups relies on using the free MAP Toolkit, which you've already seen in `Chapter 1`, *Accelerating Hyper-V Deployment*. MAP collects performance counters of all the relevant components for a Hyper-V setup. As it is used to determine your Hyper-V sizing, it can be also used in the same way to create a performance baseline of your Hyper-V setup. This can also be achieved using Microsoft **System Center Operations Manager** (**SCOM**). If you already have SCOM in place, this tool should be preferred over MAP. Refer to `Chapter 8`, *Management with System Center and Azure*, for details.

Both tools continuously read performance counters from Hyper-V hosts and their VMs and archive them in a database. Run these tasks for a continuous period-I recommend a full month-to establish an adequate baseline. In this time, you will collect the minimum, maximum, and average performance counters of your systems. The minimum values give you no real sizing information; however, the average value delivers great information for basic sizing, and the maximum values allow you to determine the factor in the peak performance of the systems.

A real value can also be drawn from the 95-percentile values for CPU, RAM, disk, and networking performance counter to plan for a solid baseline. The 95 percentiles have been proven to be a reliable source for performance measurement and sizing.

The same performance counter used by the MAP Toolkit and SCOM to create these reports can be manually tracked and tuned using **Windows Performance Monitor** (`perfmon.exe`).

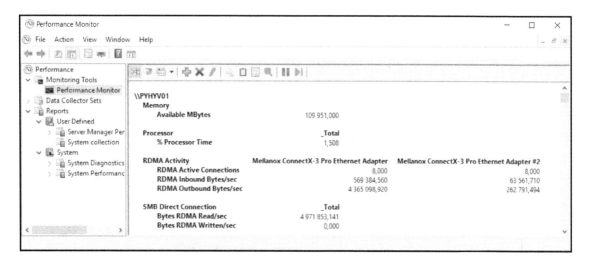

Performance monitor

Performance counter

Let's have a look at the most important performance counters for Hyper-V; you can easily access them from `perfmon.exe`.

The following basic counters are important at the host level until otherwise noted, but most of them can be used at the VM level as well.

Disk performance

Having enough capacity in your storage is important, but, as we saw earlier, storage in a datacenter is all about IOPS. There are two important performance counters telling us that there are not enough IOPS available: `\Logical Disk(*)\Avg. sec/Read` and `\Logical Disk(*)\Avg. sec/Write`.

These measure the disk latency of the systems following a shortage of IOPS. If the storage subsystem provides enough IOPS, the latencies for read and write storage performances should not go beyond 15 milliseconds.

A disk latency between 15 and 25 milliseconds, or even higher, can cause a negative impact on the performance of your VMs and applications, and a disk latency over 25 milliseconds will cause a negative impact for sure. High disk latency is the number one reason for slow Hyper-V performance, because design for storage IOPS is often neglected.

Use the individual disk counter to filter this setting to a specific disk level. Be aware while using logical disks from a SAN or NAS, because this counter only leverages the whole logical disk and not the individual physical disks.

Memory performance

To check whether enough memory is available inside a VM or at the Hyper-V host level, use the following two performance counters:

- `\Memory\Available Mbytes`: This measures the RAM available for running the active processes. Make sure that at least 15 percent of the maximum installed memory is available. If this is not the case, add more RAM to the physical host or virtual machine. If you use dynamic memory inside a virtual machine, make sure that you increase the buffer to make more RAM available to the virtual machine.

- `\Memory\Pages/sec`: This counter measures the rate of how often the disk is accessed to resolve hard page faults. To achieve this, the operating system swaps the contents of memory to the disks, which affects the performance notably. Make sure that this counter stays below 500 pages per second; otherwise, this is a clear indicator that your system needs more RAM.

Network performance

Again, here are the two most important performance counters to measure the Hyper-V network performance:

- `\Network Interface(*)\Bytes Total/sec`: This counter measures the amount of current network utilization. Subtract this from the total network bandwidth available, and make sure that you get at least 20 percent of the remaining network bandwidth available.

- `\Network Interface(*)\Output Queue Length`: This counter measures the latency in sending network packets in the form of threads that wait on the NIC. This queue should always be zero; a value higher than 1 is a sign of degraded network performance.

To measure the network utilization on the guest operating systems, use the `\Hyper-V Virtual Network Adapter(*)\Bytes/sec` counter to identify which virtual network adapters are consuming the most network utilization.

RDMA and SMB Direct performance

If you have implemented a solution based on SMB 3, you should be interested in the RDMA and SMB 3 performance counter:

- \RDMA Activity: These counters show you the global activity related to RDMA. You can see, for example, the number of RDMA inbound or outbound bytes/sec, the number of active connections, and so on.
- \SMB Direct Connection: These counters measure information related to SMB Direct such as the number of bytes RDMA read or wrote per second.

Processor performance

Last but not least, here are the two top performance counters to measure the CPU performance at the host level:

- \Processor(*)\% Processor Time: This counter is only applicable at the host level and measures the overall CPU utilization. This counter should not exceed 80 percent in a good performance baseline
- \Hyper-V Hypervisor Logical Processor(_Total)\% Total Run Time: This counter is used at the host level to evaluate a guest operating system processor

To identify the CPU power used by the host itself, use the Hyper-V Hypervisor Root Virtual Processor - % Total Run Time counter.

You already learned about the \Hyper-V Hypervisor Logical Processor(_Total)\% Total Run Time counter at the host level. There is another counter that is very similar to this one: Hyper-V Hypervisor Virtual Processor(_Total)\% Total Run Time.

It is also run at the host level, but it leverages the amount of virtual processors you gave to each virtual machine and not the leveraged logical processors at the host level. This allows you to receive valuable sizing information. If the logical processor counter is high but the virtual processor counter is low, it means that you have allocated more vCPUs to VMs than physically available.

The \Hyper-V Hypervisor Virtual Processor(*)\%Guest Run Time counter allows you to identify which vCPUs are consuming the logical CPU resources to find a suitable candidate for deallocation.

Performance tuning

After establishing performance counter baselines, it's time to interpret them. The values of networking, disks, and memory are self-explanatory, so let's go into the details of CPU sizing.

If the logical processor counter is low, but the virtual processor counter is high, it means that you can add more vCPUs to your virtual machines, as the logical processors are still available.

Theoretically, there is really no upper limit to how many virtual CPUs you can assign to virtual machines. The Microsoft recommendation is to not exceed more than 8 virtual CPUs per physical CPU core for server workloads and more than 12 virtual CPUs per physical CPU core for VDI workloads. However, there is no support limit, and there are low-workload scenarios where this recommendation can be extended.

My real-world experience from working with performance counters and baselines is to use a 1:4 ratio for production workload as a rule of thumb and a 1:12 ratio for Test/VDI workloads as a sizing baseline.

Keep in mind that a virtual machine with four vCPUs can actually be slower than the same VM with only two vCPUs, because waiting for four available threads on the host can take longer than waiting for two. That's why you should attach only necessary vCPUs to virtual machines and also avoid over-commitment at the guest level.

Hyper-V power options and green IT

Windows Server with Hyper-V is optimized for performance as well as for green IT in the default configuration. Achieving both the targets at the same time is a trade-off. It is a trade-off for using nearly the best performance when needed while saving as much power as possible. Hyper-V supports a lot of power-saving options, such as CPU core parking or changing processor speeds, but not all of them. Standby mode and hibernation are not possible on a Hyper-V host. I recommend a green-IT approach. About two-thirds of all the costs of a server, in its typical life span, are generated from operating costs such as those for the cooling and the power of the system, and only one-third falls back on the initial costs of the server hardware itself. So, saving power is a very important factor when running IT infrastructures.

I have seen Hyper-V losing some benchmarks against other virtualization products, and on rare occasions, I have experienced performance trade-offs due to this green-IT-oriented behavior. By extracting the last few performance points of Hyper-V, but not caring about saving energy, it is possible to change this default behavior positioned on the power options of Hyper-V hosts.

A Windows Server installation, either at a physical or virtual level, will use the balanced power scheme by default. After switching this performance plan to high performance, I have seen better performance and lower latency on Hyper-V hosts with up to 10 percent difference. At the guest OS level (where a change in the power options does not have an effect), I have seen SQL databases perform up to 20 percent better when the underlying host uses the high-performance power plan.

I recommend that you use the following best practices:

- Leave the lab-utilized, test-utilized, and low-utilized Hyper-V hosts on the default *balanced* power plan.
- Switch the power plan on typically utilized production hosts to *high performance*
- Leave the guest VM power plan on *balanced*
- Also, when running benchmarks against the other guys, make sure that you have the host power setting on high performance
- Change the power plan on the Hyper-V host to high performance by starting an elevated shell, and run the following command:

```
POWERCFG.EXE /S SCHEME_MIN
```

Don't get confused; SCHEME_MIN does not refer to minimum performance but to minimum power saving. It has the CPU turbo frequencies always enabled, and it disables core parking.

After that, the GUI will represent the setting, as shown in the following screenshot:

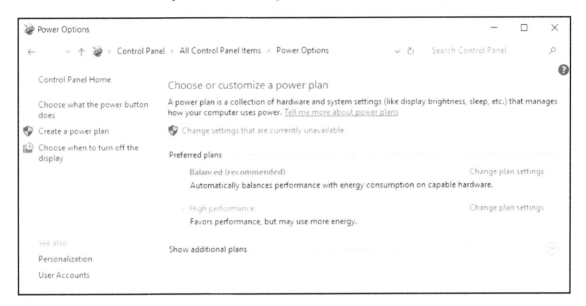

Power options

To revert to the balanced power scheme, use `POWERCFG.EXE /S SCHEME_BALANCED`.

Whatever power plan you use, make sure that you use high-efficiency power supplies and fans of variable speed in your servers to save as much energy and money as possible.

Hardware-tuning options

There are several options available to get more performance out of your Hyper-V hosts, starting with hardware features and going over hypervisor and driver configurations up to application tuning and usage scenarios. Let's start with the hardware options by selecting high-performance hardware for our Hyper-V host.

Adding more CPUs and cores as well as selecting processors with Hyper-V threading benefits the VM ratio that our host can handle. Choosing CPUs with bigger caches improve the overall Hyper-V performance. As of early 2016, Intel offers CPUs with 55 MB smart cache, but they are nearly 7,000 USD far away from being as cheap as Intel's mainstream CPUs for virtualization.

Using CPUs with **Second Level Address Translation** (**SLAT**) is not required for server operating systems (for client operating systems, it is) but is highly recommended. SLAT is also required for VDI workloads. Adding SLAT options such as **Extended Page Tables** (**EPT**) or **Nested Page Tables** (**NPT**) increases the overall Hyper-V performance. To take it further, choose CPUs with a higher frequency. Intel's Xeon E7v3 CPUs deliver up to 3.2 GHz frequency with the option to auto-increase up to 3.5 GHz per core. A core with doubled frequency typically provides better performance over two cores with a single frequency. Multiple cores do not provide a perfect scaling; they provide lesser scaling if hyper-threading is enabled because hyper-threading relies on sharing resources of the same physical core.

There are only two supported CPU vendors for Hyper-V hosts as of today-Intel and AMD. I have tested both and was unable to detect a performance benefit for either one, so choose the vendor of your choice/price point. In my experience, AMD offers a little more performance per euro/dollar, while most of my Hyper-V customers use a standardized Intel setup for all workloads. Just make sure not to mix both vendors in your Hyper-V deployment, and you will be fine.

In terms of memory, you have already learned that a pagefile does not require any special configuration. Also, the amount of RAM needed by the Hyper-V host is determined and configured automatically, so you can focus on the needs of the virtual machines on the RAM configuration. In a hyperconverged scenario, be careful of the RAM that will be used for virtual machines and for storage, especially when you implement a lot of storage cache. In this scenario, for each 1 TB of cache, 10 GB of RAM will be used.

Do not use traditional PCI slots on your servers anymore; PCIe offers greatly enhanced performance. Make sure that you use PCIe v3.0 x8 and higher slots for 10-gigabit Ethernet adapters on the server's mainboard to not limit performance at this physical level.

If you have enough adapter slots available on your server system, use multiple NICs with fewer slots instead of single NICs with many ports for optimal performance and redundancy.

Network-hardware-tuning options

Choosing the right network hardware for your Hyper-V hosts can boost up your overall VM performance. There are several hardware features available for supporting the Hyper-V host. You have already read about SMB Direct with RDMA-capable network cards, but there are many more offload capabilities.

Receive Side Scaling (RSS)

RSS is an NIC-driver technology that enables the efficient distribution of a network that receives processing across multiple CPUs in multiprocessor systems. This basically means that whenever you are not using RSS, all the CPU requests to control Hyper-V networking are delivered to the first CPU core. Even if you have four physical CPUs with 12 cores each and with hyper-threading enabled, only the very first core receives these requests. If you use network bandwidths faster than 4 GB/s, there is a high possibility that you will receive a performance hit when not using RSS. So, make sure that it's available on your NIC, and on your NIC-driver and is activated. If this is the case, these network requests (interrupts) will be spread among all the available CPU cores.

RSS is only available on the physical host, but not inside virtual machines. Windows Server 2012 R2 offers a solution for this-**Dynamic Virtual Machine Queue (D-VMQ)**. With D-VMQ enabled on our hosts, *we can use RSS on our virtual machines*.

To see if your adapters are ready for D-VMQ, check via PowerShell:

```
Get-NetAdapterVmq -Name NICName
```

Enable vRSS in one VM via PowerShell:

```
Enable-NetAdapterRSS -Name NICName
```

In Windows Server 2012 R2, vRSS didn't work on virtual NICs attached to the virtual switch on the host management partition. Thanks to SET described in `Chapter 5`, *Network Best Practices*, we can now leverage vRSS in the management partition. However, several features are not available when using SET such as **Single root I/O virtualization (SR-IOV)**. So you have to choose which one is the best for you. To use vRSS in your VMs, it's necessary to use D-VMQ at the host level.

The following screenshot shows the Hyper-V guest with vRSS:

```
Name                                           : Management-0
InterfaceDescription                           : Microsoft Hyper-V Network Adapter
Enabled                                        : True
NumberOfReceiveQueues                          : 2
Profile                                        : NUMAStatic
BaseProcessor: [Group:Number]                  : 0:0
MaxProcessor: [Group:Number]                   : 0:1
MaxProcessors                                  : 2
RssProcessorArray: [Group:Number/NUMA Distance] : 0:0/0  0:1/0
IndirectionTable: [Group:Number]               : 0:0    0:1    0:0    0:1    0:0    0:1    0:0    0:1
                                                 0:0    0:1    0:0    0:1    0:0    0:1    0:0    0:1
                                                 0:0    0:1    0:0    0:1    0:0    0:1    0:0    0:1
                                                 0:0    0:1    0:0    0:1    0:0    0:1    0:0    0:1
                                                 0:0    0:1    0:0    0:1    0:0    0:1    0:0    0:1
                                                 0:0    0:1    0:0    0:1    0:0    0:1    0:0    0:1
                                                 0:0    0:1    0:0    0:1    0:0    0:1    0:0    0:1
                                                 0:0    0:1    0:0    0:1    0:0    0:1    0:0    0:1
                                                 0:0    0:1    0:0    0:1    0:0    0:1    0:0    0:1
                                                 0:0    0:1    0:0    0:1    0:0    0:1    0:0    0:1
                                                 0:0    0:1    0:0    0:1    0:0    0:1    0:0    0:1
                                                 0:0    0:1    0:0    0:1    0:0    0:1    0:0    0:1
                                                 0:0    0:1    0:0    0:1    0:0    0:1    0:0    0:1
```

vRSS information in a Hyper-V guest OS

Single Root IO Virtualization

SR-IOV is another great capability in Hyper-V networking. It allows for a PCIe device, such as an NIC, to be presented to multiple devices, such as virtual machines. Think of it as PCIe virtualization. This only works when it is supported at a physical level (network card), on the server system (BIOS), as well as on Hyper-V. SR-IOV offers more performance than VMQ because it uses **Direct memory access** (**DMA**) for direct communication between the physical NIC and the virtual machine. All the other aspects of Hyper-V networking are bypassed so that there is no involvement of NIC Teaming, virtual switches, and other technologies on top of it. This allows for extremely low latency and will be a great option when Hyper-V network virtualization causes CPU impacts through RSS without DMQ, otherwise. However, this also means that if you use NIC Teaming, these NICs cannot be used for SR-IOV, and there is no vSwitch in between that allows for Quality of Service or other management. SR-IOV is compatible with live migration and other Hyper-V features that do not involve network virtualization.

In my experience, SR-IOV is a great choice when handling low-latency, high-bandwidth VMs (for example, VoIP communication) and should be used when the traditional networking model, without SR-IOV, does not deliver enough networking performance. However, it should not be your default option because of the decreased management capabilities.

There is a great blog series about SR-IOV by Microsoft's John Howard available at `http://b` `it.ly/1uvyagL`.

Other offload capabilities

Checksum calculation on your NICs can offload the calculation and validation of the TCP and UDP checksums as well as the IPv4 and IPv6 adapters. This feature should be available and activated on all used network adapters with Hyper-V.

When using network traffic encryption with IPSec, you should use the IPSec offload; otherwise, you will see a 20-30 percent performance hit on your Hyper-V CPUs. However, you should use IPSec only when the security standards of your company tell you to, unless you leave them disabled.

Jumbo frames are another great option to boost network traffic; however, they need end-to-end configuration to work properly. On the physical NICs of the Hyper-V host, configure jumbo frames according to the packet size. The recommendation for most Intel NICs, for example, is an MTU of 9014 bytes. While jumbo frames don't need any configuration on the Hyper-V vSwitch, they need to be configured on the physical switch port as well as on the guest OS NIC. After configuration, you can test your configuration easily using the `ping` command with huge packet sizes:

```
ping -f -l 8500 192.168.1.10
```

It's best practice to enable jumbo frames if they are supported by all parts of the chain. It is also compatible with most of the Hyper-V networking features such as RSS, and I highly recommend that you enable it when using ISCSI storage as well.

There are other offloading features, such as **Receive-Segment Coalescing** (**RSC**), that reduce the number of IP headers; however, they do not bring any more notable performance benefits to Hyper-V VMs and are therefore not explained further. Moreover, this offloading feature is not supported in Switch Embedded Teaming.

For additional details on these features or other advanced Hyper-V network-related performance tunings, visit the network section of *Windows Server Performance Tuning Guidelines* found at `http://bit.ly/1rNpTkR`.

Using IPv6 with Hyper-V

Another common question is about the use of the modern IP protocol, IPv6. It is enabled by default on Windows Server 2016 with Hyper-V, and you better leave it this way. The entire Windows development is done and tested with IPv6 enabled. There can be unforeseen problems occurring after disabling IPv6.

However, if your network standard dictates that you disable IPv6, it can be done on the Hyper-V host as well on the VMs. If you decide to disable IPv6, do it only in the registry. We will add the corresponding registry key via PowerShell:

```
New-ItemProperty
"HKLM:\SYSTEM\CurrentControlSet\Services\Tcpip6\Parameters" -
    Name "DisabledComponents" -Value 0xffffffff -PropertyType "DWord"
```

Then, reboot the system. Don't use any other method to disable IPv6, such as unchecking the checkbox in the TCP IP properties of the network card; I've seen problems occurring after that.

I have seen many customers disabling IPv6 via the registry, and some of them had issues with other roles such as Windows Server RRAS. However, I have not seen a single customer experiencing problems with the Hyper-V role with a registry-disabled IPv6. So, you are fine until now with this configuration, but it's still not recommended by Microsoft.

Storage tuning options

In the earlier chapters, you got an overview of the great storage options possible with Hyper-V. Let's now focus on some additional performance tuning for storage. You have seen how dynamically expanding hard disks are a great option for flexibility, especially in combination with thin provisioning, which is supported by Hyper-V on a software-based and hardware-based level. Hyper-V has some special features for the other way around, then data gets deleted. It is important to let the storage subsystem know that the blocks occupied previously are now ready for reuse. If this did not happen, the physical storage system would consider itself full of data, while on a logical level, it would be half empty. In a worst-case situation, you will be unable to write to a nonfull drive. Windows Server with Hyper-V uses standardized Trim and Unmap functions.

They are enabled by default and don't need any configuration, but you should make sure that your used storage is capable of working with the Trim/Unmap functions to maximize storage efficiency. Only Hyper-V-SCSI, an enlightened IDE, and virtual FC controllers allow the unmap command from the guest to reach the host virtual-storage stack. On the virtual hard disks, only virtual disks formatted as VHDX support unmap commands from the guest. This is another reason to use VHDX files. If you are working with generation 1 VMs, make sure that you use a small IDE-attached system partition and a VHDX file on a SCSI controller for data and applications.

Windows Server with Hyper-V enables a lot of background jobs to consolidate and optimize storage, such as deduplication and defrag jobs. To ensure that these jobs work flawlessly, make sure that you keep at least 10 percent of free space on all drives, including cluster-shared volumes.

Offloaded Data Transfer

Offloaded Data Transfer (**ODX**) is a great way of speeding up data transfers. If you use an ODX-capable storage, Windows Server with Hyper-V will check, before starting a copy job whether there is a faster approach than copying the data on the software stack. It passes a token to the storage subsystem of the copy source and target, and if both tokens are received by an ODX-capable storage system, the copy job will be done at a hardware-assisted level. If the source and target occur on the same system, no data will be copied; instead a new link to the same blocks will be created in just a few seconds.

The Hyper-V storage stack also issues ODX operations during maintenance operations for VHDs, such as merging disks after deleting a snapshot.

ODX is enabled by default; however, it is again only supported on virtual hard disks that are attached to an SCSI controller. An IDE controller does not support this feature. Also, if your storage subsystem does not support ODX for Windows Server 2016, you should disable it via PowerShell in the registry, as I have seen problems in this combination:

```
Set-ItemProperty HKLM:\SYSTEM\CurrentControlSet\Control\FileSystem `
            -Name "FilterSupportedFeaturesMode" `
            -Value 1
```

Then, reboot the system after setting the key.

Even if your storage subsystem supports ODX, make sure that you test it before using it in production.

Shutdown tuning options

There are some additional options to tune the performance of Hyper-V and its VMs; these options are listed in this section.

Setting the shutdown timeout

If you use a Hyper-V cluster and you send a `shutdown` command to one of its nodes, the node will immediately start a live migration of all the running VMs on this node to free up the node. If you send a `shutdown` command to a standalone host, it tries to shut down all the VMs. However, it is possible that a cluster node starts rebooting while live migrations and VM shutdown operations are still in progress. This host shutdown time can be configured via the registry. Perform the following steps:

1. Open **regedit**
2. Navigate to **HKLM\Cluster**
3. Edit the **ShutdownTimeoutInMinutes** value according to your needs
4. Reboot the system after setting the key

It might take some experimenting to find out the right value for you; I typically set it no higher than 10 minutes.

Hyper-V benchmarking

After successfully establishing some performance baselines for Hyper-V, it's important to create regular benchmarks of your Hyper-V environment. Use MAP or SCOM to monitor the performance of the common performance counters, but I recommend that you use an overall benchmark from time to time to make sure that the performance on the application level is consistent.

Which type of benchmark you use depends on your workload. I highly recommend a standardized benchmark that utilizes a database and an application tier. The primary benchmark for this is the SAP SD benchmark. If you are a SAP customer, this is the way to go. You can find a Microsoft blog post about a SAP Hyper-V reference benchmark at `http:/ /bit.ly/1nMVSQw`.

If you do not use SAP or another ERP system with this type of benchmark, you can use other available benchmarks. I highly recommend **PassMark Performance Test**, which is available for a 30-day trial at `http://bit.ly/UFd2Ff`, because it offers benchmarks that utilize all of the hardware resources discussed. I also recommend SQLIO to test the storage and storage connections available at `http://bit.ly/1obVdIV`. If you want to use desktop virtualization, you can use the **Login VSI** benchmark; to find out more, check out `http://bit.ly/1pt2roe`. To finish, Microsoft has released a Powershell set to evaluate the overall IOPS of the storage solution. This tool is called **VM Fleet**. For further information, check out `http://bit.ly/2bfhPJU`.

The results from all these benchmarks are comparable to other Hyper-V setups as well as to other virtualization platforms that do not utilize Hyper-V performance counters.

Hyper-V for virtual desktops

Most of the time, Hyper-V is used to host virtual machines with server operating systems installed. Hyper-V also offers great capabilities for hosting virtual desktops, but because special licensing is needed, Hyper-V VDI implementations are not seen very often. This topic focuses on using Hyper-V with virtual desktops and its tuning for client operating systems.

Be aware that a VDI deployment is, in most cases, not cheaper than a deployment of remote desktop session hosts (Terminal Services), but can offer a standardized architecture with a central point of management.

To create a hosting infrastructure for virtual desktops, use the server manager on an existing Windows Server 2016. The **Add Roles** wizard has a full VDI deployment wizard on board. Of course, you can alternatively use PowerShell to install a full VDI environment:

```
    New-RDVirtualDesktopDeployment -ConnectionBroker
VDI01.int.homecloud.net -
    WebAccessServer VDI02.int.homecloud.net -VirtualizationHost
    VDI03.int.homecloud.net
```

There is also a great end-to-end PowerShell solution available for implementing a VDI scenario in a lab and also for teaching all the necessary PowerShell cmdlets for the VDI setup.

The **Virtual Desktop Infrastructure Starter Kit** (**VDI SK**) is created by Microsoft's Victor Arzate and is available in the Technet gallery at `http://bit.ly/1pkILFP`.

The quick-start setup installs all the VDI-related services on a single operating system instance; this is not recommended in any case. In both cases, a virtual-based desktop deployment is necessary for VDI. Configure the target server for each of the VDI workloads:

- **Remote Desktop Connection Broker**: The RD Connection Broker connects or reconnects a client device to the VDI client (virtual machine)
- **Remote Desktop Web Access**: The RD Web Access server enables users to connect to its VDI client through session collections and virtual desktop collections, using the web browser
- **Remote Desktop Session Host**: The RD Session Host is a VDI-enabled Hyper-V host

After entering the server names, the further configuration will be done by Server Manager/PowerShell without any need for manual configuration.

If you already have a Hyper-V-ready environment, start by creating a VM template for VDI. Install a new Hyper-V VM with the client operating system of your choice (I highly recommend at least Windows 8.1 because of its improved VDI features) as the *Golden Image*.

After finishing the installation of Windows, including all the updates and support tools you want to have in every VDI client, run Sysprep with the OOBE/generalize option and choose to shut down the system:

```
C:\Windows\System32\Sysprep\Sysprep.exe /OOBe /Generalize /Shutdown
/Mode:VM
```

Using the new `/Mode:VM` switch allows for a faster sysprep, as there is a lot less hardware recognizing for virtual machines necessary as long as you are using the same virtualization environment.

Copy the source VM and specify its path in the next script.

To create a new virtual desktop collection, use the following PowerShell script:

```
New-RDVirtualDesktopCollection -CollectionName demoPool -PooledManaged
`
 -VirtualDesktopTemplateName WinGold.vhdx `
 -VirtualDesktopTemplateHostServer VDI01 `
 -VirtualDesktopAllocation @{$Servername = 1} `
 -StorageType LocalStorage `
 -ConnectionBroker VDI02 `
 -VirtualDesktopNamePrefix msVDI
```

Licensing hint

Microsoft uses special licensing around VDI (VDA licenses). If you already have your Hyper-V hosts covered by the datacenter editions of Windows Server, it can be more economical for you to just use single-user-server VMs instead of real-client VMs.

Some great performance white papers on VDI are available in project VRC at `http://bit.l y/1nwr9aK`; they measure the impact of an antivirus or Microsoft Office in a VDI environment.

Using RemoteFX

Microsoft's **Remote Desktop Protocol** (**RDP**) is currently available in Version 8.1 or later and offers great capabilities, including RemoteFX. A little-known fact is that the RDP native client is available for a broad range of platforms, including Windows 7, Windows 8, Windows 8.1, Windows RT, Windows Phone, and also Android and Apple iOS.

RemoteFX offers some great features around RDP connections, and almost all of them can be used without special graphic adapters. RemoteFX is enabled by default and offers features such as multitouch, adaptive graphics, and WAN optimization. The new RDP client also offers features such as automatic network detection and RDP over UDP.

RemoteFX is able to detect content by default and load it by priority. The text is loaded first, then the images are loaded, and at last, the videos and ad banners are loaded onto the screen. With these capabilities, RDP is not only more efficient, but the performance felt by the user is also significantly improved.

RemoteFX features can be configured via Group Policy as follows:

1. Open the **Group Policy Management Editor** and navigate to
   ComputerConfiguration I **AdministrativeTemplates** I **WindowsComponents** I
   Remote Desktop Services I **Remote Desktop Session Host** I **Remote Session
   Environment**:

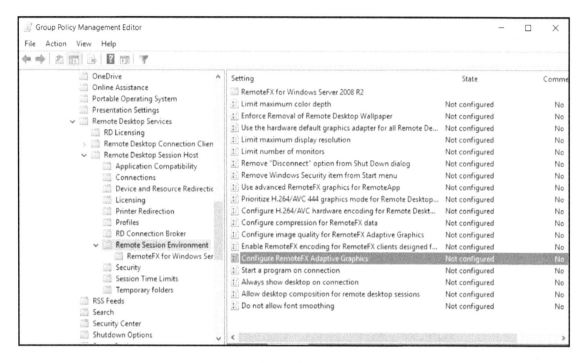

RemoteFX GPO rules

2. Edit the **Configure image quality for RemoteFX Adaptive Graphics** setting.

   Change it from **Default Medium** to **High** or **Lossless** if you want to use
   better graphics. This will consume more bandwidth.

3. Edit the **Configure RemoteFX Adaptive Graphics** setting in the same path.

   Choose **RemoteFX** to optimize between server scalability or bandwidth
   usage.

4. Edit the **Configure compression for RemoteFX data** setting in the same path.

   Choose one of **Optimize to use less memory** (which will require more network), **Optimize to use less network bandwidth** (which requires more memory), balances memory and network bandwidth, and does not use an RDP-compression algorithm. It's highly recommend to use the last option.

5. Edit the **Limit maximum color depth** setting.

   Select 32 bits per pixel. In my experience, this offers the best performance.

6. Reboot the servers.

These GPOs must be linked to the virtualization hosts, not the virtual desktops or RDSH-VMs that run on top of the virtualization hosts.

There are some other group policies available, but the default settings for them are, most of the time, just fine.

Another way to speed up RDP performance is by adding a powerful GPU to the server. High-end graphic adapters, formerly known only in gaming PCs and CAD workstations, are now available for VDI clients and RDSH VMs.

RemoteFX has been enhanced in Windows Server 2016. Now RemoteFX supports Gen 2 VM, 4K resolution, OpenGL and OpenCL API and Microsoft has improved performance.

You need to choose a GPO that supports DirectX 11.0 or higher and uses a WDDM 1.2 driver or higher. Make sure that you check the Windows Server Catalog again for RemoteFX GPUs. I have had a good experience with NVIDIA GRID adapters in terms of performance and compatibility. Also, make sure that your Hyper-V host server hardware is capable of running high-end GPUs. The typical server GPU offers only very limited performance and is only using a few of MBs of RAM. RemoteFX GPUs offer great performance and come with gigabytes of graphics RAM. When you want to do more in your VDI VMs or RDSH sessions, then just view the web pages and edit the office files; an RFX GPU might be the right option. It is suitable for running full HD videos or editing CAD models inside a virtual machine. With Hyper-V on Windows Server 2016, you can even share a GPU between numerous virtual machines. To add a GPU to a virtual machine, use the following PowerShell cmdlet:

```
Add-VMRemoteFx3dVideoAdapter -VMName VM01
```

To specify the resolution you want to use inside the VM, use the following PowerShell cmdlet:

```
SET-VMRemoteFx3dVideoAdapter -VMName VM01 -MaximumResolution 1920x1200
```

When using RemoteFX adapters with VDI VMs, it's best practice to calculate the increased memory usage. A Windows 10 VMs should then be deployed with the possibility to use up to 4 GB of RAM. In a nonRemoteFX vGPU scenario, 2 GB of RAM is enough in most scenarios. VDI clients with Windows 10 work well with dynamic memory and two CPU cores, so this should be the default setup. I often see VDI workloads deployed with differencing disks. This isn't optimal from a performance point of view, and additionally, this is a management nightmare as VMM cannot work with differencing disks. It's a far better option to use dynamic VHDX files and to activate the Windows integrated deduplication, which you learned in `Chapter 4`, *Storage Best Practices*.

Other than that, virtual machines that run a VDI workload are just another bunch of Hyper-V VMs.

Common configuration mistakes

In some of Hyper-V infrastructures where I have worked to solve performance and stability issues, I have seen the same kind of misconfiguration several times. In this section, I have tried to describe the common configuration mistakes I have seen.

Design misjudged

The first common mistake I see in Hyper-V deployment is the underestimation of the design phase. A lot of projects where I was involved didn't start by studying the existing environment. How can you know the required numbers of CPUs, memory, and storage without inspecting the current infrastructure? If you do not check out the existing environment, your new Hyper-V infrastructure might not match the requirements or could be too large (and so too expensive) with regard to your needs. Before buying hardware, run a Microsoft Assessment and Planning toolkit to calculate the required number of cores, memories, and storage capacity. Once it is calculated, you can add more resources to handle future additional VMs.

For example, currently, you have an infrastructure with 500 VMs which consumes each 2vCPU, 8 GB of RAM and 60 GB of storage. Assume that we want a consolidation rate of 4:1. To calculate the number of the required resources, we can use the following formula:

- **Cores**: *((500VM x 2vCPU) / Consolidation Rate of 4) = 250* Cores
- **RAM**: *500VM x 8 GB = 4000 GB*
- **Storage**: *500VM x 60 GB = 30 TB*

Now we have the required number to support the current workloads. But what about the future workloads that will come in the next three years? To calculate for future workloads, I assume that the infrastructure will handle 25% more VMs. Let's take the calculator again:

- **Cores**: *250 Cores x 25% = 312.5* round up to 320 Cores
- **RAM**: *4000 GB x 25% = 5 TB*
- **Storage**: *30 TB x 25% = 37.5* round up to 40 TB

For the compute and memory resources, we need the 320 Cores and the 5 TB of memory in case a node fails in the cluster. For this design, I choose the Intel x2660v4 which has 14 cores. Because each server has two CPUs, each of them has 28 Cores. So I need 348 cores to support one node failure. To calculate the number of servers, you can use this formula:

- **Number of servers**: *348 cores / 28 cores per server = 12.42* round up to 13 servers

Now that we have the number of servers, we can calculate how much memory we have to implement in each server:

- **RAM per server**: *((5000 GB / 13) + 5000 GB) / 13 = 414 GB*

This formula takes into consideration a node failure. The beginning of the formula calculates the required RAM amount per server. Then this value is added to the total amount of RAM and divided by the number of nodes. Because it is not possible to implement 414 GB of RAM in a real server, the preceding value must be rounded off to 512 GB (16 * 32 GB of RAM). With Intel Xeon v4 family, the number of memory sticks should be a multiple of four (Quad Channel) for best performance.

Therefore, to implement this example, you need 13 servers composed of two Intel Xeon 2660v4 and 16 * 32 GB of RAM.

Network teaming

I have seen some designs where a member of a teaming belonged to the same network adapter. Some network adapters can have two or even four controllers. This means that you can plug as much cable as the controller. However, even if you add all network controllers to the same team, this is not ensuring a high availability in case of a hardware issue. If there is a problem on the network adapter PCB or in the PCI-E bus, all adapters related to this one are disconnected.

This is why, in the production server, I recommend that you buy at least two different network adapters. If you need two 40 GB NICs, buy two single controller network adapters and team them. This statement is true for all network adapters and all HBA to connect to the SAN.

Another mistake I see concerns the NIC Teaming of different network adapters model. I recommend to not do this because of instability with this kind of configuration. Team together only same network adapters (same model and same firmware).

To finish, avoid creating several virtual switches and prefer leveraging network convergence. Let's think about a DMZ and a LAN network. A single virtual switch can easily handle both networks if you configure the physical switch in the trunk mode. On the other hand, if you create several virtual switches, you require several NICs and the management is less flexible.

Storage configuration

In some environments, I have seen the network adapters dedicated for iSCSI in a teaming. There is no advantage to using this configuration over MPIO. MPIO handles the network high availability and spreads the iSCSI workloads across all iSCSI NICs. So, don't use NIC Teaming for this usage.

Regarding HBA FC, I have seen some customers who mix Hyper-V storage traffic and NPIV usage. It is not an issue, but I do not recommend mixing the storage traffic and the NPIV on a single HBA to connect LUN to VM.

Operating system maintenance

During the lifecycle of the Hyper-V infrastructure, a lot of people may work on the Hyper-V OS. Sometimes they can have an issue and install a tool in a node of the cluster. Sometimes, because of lack of time, some updates are installed on one node and not on the others. Each node of the cluster not being the same is a mistake.

First, avoid installing a tool to a server. Prefer a portable tool (such as SysInternal) to troubleshoot issues. If you install an agent on a server, this agent should be deployed in each node.

Next, each node in a cluster should be at the same update level. This means that each node must have the same applied updates. By following these best practices, your cluster will be more reliable. This statement doesn't concern only Microsoft updates but also firmware and drivers. Microsoft updates can be managed through WSUS, SCCM, or SCVMM.

To avoid the installation of extra tools and to limit the number of updates to apply, I recommend that you install your Hyper-V nodes in core mode installation. Some software prevents the use of core mode installation. In such cases, you do not have the choice to deploy the nodes in full mode. But, if nothing prevents the core mode installation, prefer this mode. Whatever you choose, do not mix different installation modes in the same cluster.

Summary

By the end of this chapter, you will have implemented a lot of possible performance optimizations for your Hyper-V environment, and you don't need to fear the production usage of your setup. You will have tightened your server hardware, storage, and network as well as the Hyper-V role configuration for optimal-usage scenarios.

In Chapter 8, *Management with System Center and Azure*, you will learn more about managing your Hyper-V hosts, its virtual machines, and the complete fabric, with Microsoft's management suite, System Center. You will also learn more about the deployment, monitoring, backup, and automation of Hyper-V.

8
Management with System Center and Azure

"Every datacenter and cloud infrastructure needs an efficient management solution. With System Center, Microsoft offers a great solution for managing, automating, and monitoring your datacenter.
Especially, Virtual Machine Manager allows you to integrate your hardware resources-such as storage, networking, and compute-and manage them from a single pane of glass."

Thomas Maurer – MVP Hyper-V

Your Hyper-V environment is now configured for high performance, and you are probably expanding the use of Hyper-V by now. This chapter gives you an overview of the management of Hyper-V servers through various System Center components.

In this chapter, we will cover the following topics:

- Deployment and management with System Center Virtual Machine Manager for:
    - Service templates
    - Fabric management
    - Protecting your VM in Azure

- Monitoring with System Center Operations Manager
- Collecting and correlating data using Operational Insights
- Backup with System Center Data Protection Manager
- Automation with System Center
- Microsoft System Center

Microsoft System Center

Microsoft System Center 2016 is Microsoft's solution for advanced management of Windows Server and its components, along with its dependencies such as various hardware and software products. It consists of various components that support every stage of your IT services from planning to operating and from backup to automation. System Center has existed since 1994 and has evolved continuously. It now offers a great set of tools for very efficient management of server and client infrastructures. It also offers the ability to create and operate whole clouds-run in your own datacenter or in a public cloud datacenter such as Microsoft Azure. Today, it's your choice whether to run your workloads on-premises or off-premises. System Center provides a standardized set of tools for a unique and consistent Cloud OS management experience.

System Center does not add any new features to Hyper-V, but it does offer great ways to make the most out of it and ensure streamlined operating processes after its implementation. System Center is licensed via the same model as Windows Server, leveraging Standard and datacenter Editions on a physical host level. While every System Center component offers great value in itself, the binding of multiple components into a single workflow offers even more advantages, as shown in the following screenshot:

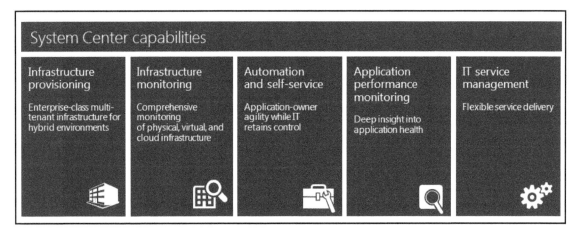

System Center overview

When do you need System Center? There is no right or wrong answer to this, and the most given answer by any IT consultant around the world is "It depends".

System Center adds value to any IT environment, starting with only a few systems. In my experience, a Hyper-V environment with up to three hosts, and 15 VMs can be managed efficiently without the use of System Center. If you plan to use more hosts or virtual machines, System Center will definitely be a great solution for you. Let's take a look at the components of System Center.

System Center Virtual Machine Manager

System Center Virtual Machine Manager (**SCVMM**) is not another hypervisor besides Hyper-V. VMM simply adds a management functionality to virtualization hosts. It works best with Hyper-V, but is also capable of managing day-to-day operational tasks for VMware vSphere through vCenter and Citrix XenServer hosts.

You can create your own virtual machine templates with VMM for fast deployment of new virtual machines with basic content and configuration. VMM takes the approach of predefined templates to a new level, by service templates. A service template not only consists of a virtual machine and a preinstalled operating system, but also offers much more, starting from the integration of software components such as databases and applications over storage to load-balanced network connections. All you need to do is define a central service template that offers dynamic expanding or shrinking of the VM environment, purely based on current performance requirements. Applications consisting of database servers, application servers, and frontend servers are ideal candidates for service templates.

There are several service templates available for download at **TechNet Gallery** (`http://bi`
`t.ly/VYK8jh`), one is shown in the following screenshot:

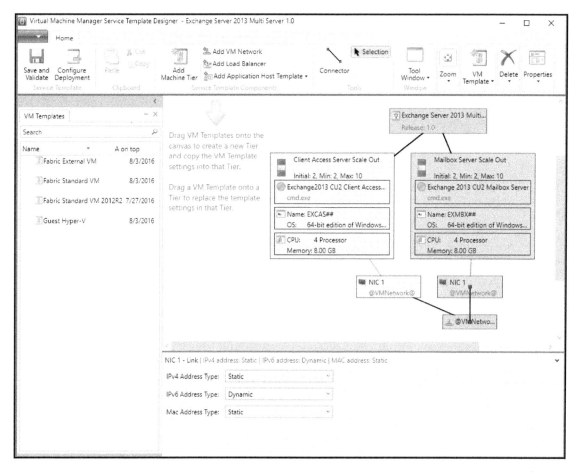

The VMM service template

SCVMM also provides full management of Fabric. Thanks to SCVMM, you can manage the Hyper-V configuration from a single pane (network, storage, Hyper-V role, and so on), manage the storage, either with a SAN (with SMI-S) or with Storage Spaces, create Hyper-V and Storage cluster, make a bare-metal provisioning of Hyper-V and storage node, and so on. SCVMM is not just a new GUI on top of the Failover Clustering manager, but a tool to manage all your Hyper-V infrastructure environment.

SCVMM can be deployed in high availability in a classical Failover Cluster. To install SCVMM in this way, you need to install and configure the Failover Clustering feature on both servers without a shared disk (except for quorum witness). Then install SCVMM, and while using the wizard, you will be asked to deploy the tool in high availability.

When you run SCVMM for the first time, I recommend that you disable the **Create logical networks automatically** option to avoid the creation of the object related to the virtual switches that you have deployed in the Hyper-V nodes. You can find this option in **Settings | General | Network settings**.

Then you should create a host group to sort the Hyper-V nodes. When I deploy SCVMM, I always try to create a first host group level, which represents the location (Lyon, Paris, New York, and so on) and a second level, which represents the Hyper-V nodes usage (hosting, NVGRE Gateway, fabric servers, and so on). It is not necessary to create a lot of levels as it will complicate the management of SCVMM. Creating host groups allow delegated and granular management.

Next, you should configure the networking in **Fabric**. If you fully manage the network in SCVMM, this can help you to provision Hyper-V, storage nodes, and VMs. The SCVMM network functionality contains a great feature called the **IP Address Pool (IP Pool)**. The IP Pool enables you to create a pool of IP addresses that can be used when you deploy Hyper-V or storage nodes and VMs.

The IP address is assigned statically in the virtual network adapter and a reservation is applied on this IP address:

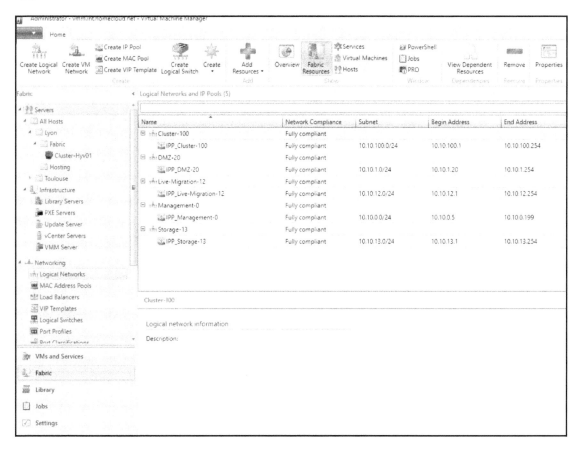

Network configuration in SCVMM

Moreover, you can configure Switch Embedded Teaming and virtual network adapter from SCVMM. When the network is configured, you are able to configure the Hyper-V nodes network adapters from SCVMM.

Once the network is configured, you can connect your storage system to SCVMM to create LUN and SMB share and have of about free spaces. Then the CSV can be sorted in storage classifications. These classifications enable you to provision a VM in a storage location belonging to the chosen storage classification. It eases the automation of VM deployment:

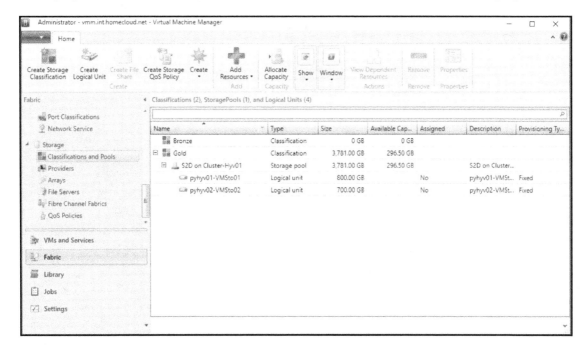

Storage management from SCVMM

SCVMM is also able to be connected to a WSUS Server (it can be the same as SCCM while WSUS is configured by SCCM). If you connect a WSUS server, you can create an update baseline and associate it to a host group and/or fabric servers. The compliance is checked and if the server is not compliant, you can remediate from SCVMM. The remediation will install the update on the server.

Then you should install a file server that will be used as a VMM library. DFS is not supported in the VMM library, but you can leverage a file server in a cluster failover. This file server will contain an ISO file, unattended xml file, or sysprep'd VHDX. This configuration is described at `http://bit.ly/1uhyrzD`. For example, I often deploy VM using the following unattended XML file:

```xml
<?xml version="1.0" encoding="utf-8"?>
<unattend xmlns="urn:schemas-microsoft-com:unattend">
    <settings pass="oobeSystem">
        <component name="Microsoft-Windows-International-Core"
        processorArchitecture="x86"
        publicKeyToken="31bf3856ad364e35" language="neutral"
        versionScope="nonSxS"
        xmlns:wcm="http://schemas.microsoft.com/WMIConfig/2002/State"
        xmlns:xsi="http://www.w3.org/2001/XMLSchema-instance">
            <InputLocale>fr-FR;en-US</InputLocale>
            <UserLocale>en-US</UserLocale>
            <UILanguageFallback>en-US</UILanguageFallback>
            <SystemLocale>en-US</SystemLocale>
            <UILanguage>en-US</UILanguage>
        </component>
    </settings>
    <settings pass="generalize">
        <component name="Microsoft-Windows-PnpSysprep"
        processorArchitecture="amd64"
        publicKeyToken="31bf3856ad364e35" language="neutral"
        versionScope="nonSxS"
        xmlns:wcm="http://schemas.microsoft.com/WMIConfig/2002/State"
        xmlns:xsi="http://www.w3.org/2001/XMLSchema-instance">
            <PersistAllDeviceInstalls>true
            </PersistAllDeviceInstalls>
        </component>
    </settings>
</unattend>
```

This answer file configures the keyboard layout of the virtual machine and does not check new hardware at VM deployment.

You can also connect Windows Deployment Services (WDS) which will be used to provision Hyper-V and/or storage node. Then the physical computer profiles will be leveraged. To provision a node from SCVMM you have to do the following:

- Connect a WDS server to SCVMM
- Create a sysprep'd VHDX with the main configuration of the operating system and copy it into the SCVMM library
- Create a physical computer profile
- Configure an IPMI account that is allowed to start, restart, and stop the computer in the Baseboard Management Controller
- Start a bare-metal provisioning and specify the IP Address (or a range) of the BMC
- Configure NIC's IP address and classification if you have not used **Consistent Device Naming (CDN)**

You can also add a post install PowerShell script in the physical computer profile. When I am involved in a Hyper-V project, I spend a lot of time on configuring this profile and scripts to provision Hyper-V automatically. PowerShell scripts are often the driver installation, the agent deployment (SCCM, SCOM, backup, and so on), and some custom configurations. For further information about provisioning Hyper-V with this method, refer to `http://bit.ly/2beBdI9`.

SCVMM also offers the capability to create Hyper-V cluster and Storage Spaces configuration. For further information, refer to `http://bit.ly/2bmeG8k`.

Once these configurations have been made, you can install the SCVMM agent in each Hyper-V node that you have already deployed to manage them from SCVMM.

If you plan to manage your Hyper-V infrastructure from SCVMM, I highly recommend that you configure just two Hyper-V nodes and deploy all the basic VMs to run SCVMM (Domain Controller, SQL Server, and VMM). Once the configuration of SCVMM is finished, you will have to migrate the network of the Hyper-V nodes and VMs from standalone managed (standard switches) to SCVMM managed (logical switches). This migration involves some network outage.

A new feature of SCVMM 2016 is the capability to upgrade a Windows Server 2012 R2 cluster to Windows Server 2016 by leveraging the Rolling Cluster Upgrade (we will discuss this feature in `Chapter 9`, *Migration to Hyper-V 2016*). This feature leverages the bare-metal provisioning feature to upgrade a cluster in Windows Server 2012 R2 to Windows Server 2016 without recreating a new cluster for the migration.

I wrote a white paper a long time ago about the *Implement a highly available Private Cloud to host Virtual Machines*. This is a step-by-step guide which also explains the configuration of SCVMM. You can download it at `http://bit.ly/2bmfs5c`.

To learn more about VMM, refer to *System Center 2012 R2 Virtual Machine Manager Cookbook*, by *Edvaldo Alessandro Cardoso*, published by *Packt Publishing*, at `http://bit.ly/1vBjf4i`.

System Center Operations Manager

System Center Operations Manager (**SCOM**) is an end-to-end monitoring tool offering a great transparency to your infrastructure. While many monitoring solutions are available in the market, there are none as sophisticated as SCOM. While other solutions monitor a given set of up to 30 parameters per host, such as checking for free space on drives, pinging systems, and checking whether a specific Windows service is running, SCOM offers far more value.

With hundreds and thousands of preconfigured rulesets monitoring your environment, delivered in management packs, OM not only detects the exact location and source of the problem but also delivers great guidance on how to work around an incident or apply a permanent solution without the need to leave the SCOM console.

These management packs are free to download for all Microsoft products and are ready to use. You don't need to put more time into configuration than into other monitoring solutions that do not offer this granularity. This great concept of an SCOM allows you to avoid many problems before there is an impact on production systems, such as receiving notifications via an instant messenger or e-mail, or creating automatic recovery tasks in the event of an error.

You can receive all relevant performance information about your systems, including Hyper-V hosts and VMs. You can also monitor the network devices and switches connected to your Hyper-V environment as well as the application-level performance of web applications such as the self-service portal. With SCOM, you can forward the collected information to your trouble-stricken system, that is, System Center Service Manager, and close the ticket when the problem gets resolved. With this great level of detail, SCOM is even capable of calculating future performance requirements based on your usage in the past.

For advanced scenarios, Microsoft's partner Veeam offers a commercial Hyper-V management pack allowing you to go even further into the Hyper-V stack from a monitoring perspective. The SCOM screen looks as follows:

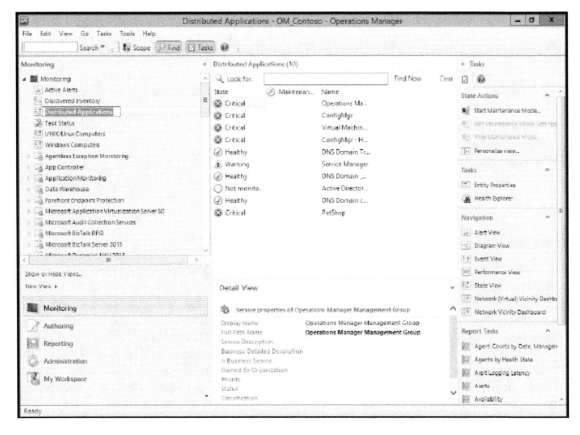

System center operations manager

Here are the main steps to get SCOM up and running:

- Install your SCOM servers. You will typically install two SCOM servers: one as your primary monitoring server and the other as the data warehouse. The installation and basic configuration are described at `http://bit.ly/1r0by4u`.
- Add SCOM agents to your Hyper-V hosts and VMs through the SCOM Discovery Wizard to enable monitoring. This configuration is described at `http://bit.ly/1uhBvMj`.
- Import the necessary Hyper-V management packs. This process is described at `http://bit.ly/VZitid`.
- Configure the override to customize enabled rules and monitors and change threshold alert.
- For additional information on SCOM, visit this virtual academy course at `http://bit.ly/1wXQkZS`.

System Center Service Manager

Microsoft's **Service Manager** (**SM**) is often described as the Microsoft version of a helpdesk tool. However, SCSM offers a lot more than that and is a fully capable IT service management tool. With SCSM, you can document incidents and problems, plan the next software release, and start document planned changes. An SCSM is the most central component where all the data comes together. Through integrated connectors, the collected data from all other System Center components are centralized in a complete **Configuration Management Database** (**CMDB**) that allows you to pull more value out of this data. Its SharePoint-based self-service portal allows for end user communication and a web-based creation of incidents and service requests. An SCSM comes with a set of built-in best practice processes for core ITIL components. ITIL and MOF are a set of best practice descriptions on IT service management processes.

By orchestrating this knowledge across the various System Center components, an SCSM helps IT staff to continuously adapt to new requirements while lowering costs and reducing time to resolution. This is the reason why an SCSM is a great tool for aligning your IT to your business needs. You can use Service-Level Agreements to proof this value with SCSM functionalities.

You can also leverage the great data resource pool to create transparent reporting for optimization, or use a chargeback or showback-based reporting for virtual machine resources. The following screenshot shows the SCSM screen:

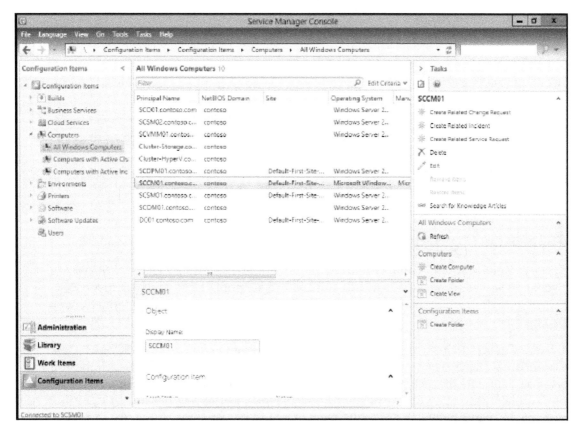

System center service manager

You can use SLA dashboards with SCSM to demonstrate the great performance of IT on the company's Intranet portal or use huge Excel spreadsheets for optimization.

SCSM offers even further value through various partner extensions from companies such as Cireson, Opslogix, and Provance, including full asset management solutions.

The main steps to get your SCSM (installation described at `http://bit.ly/1qhhQg6`) up and running are as follows:

1. Register your data warehouse server after its installation. This is described at `http://bit.ly/1pxWgEK`.
2. Deploy the self-service portal to enable end user interaction. This is described at `http://bit.ly/1Ch1wAT`.
3. Configure SCSM connectors to import data from the various System Center components to create a complete CMDB solution. This is described at `http://bit.ly/1Ch1Dwn`.

For additional information on SCSM, visit the book at `http://bit.ly/1owrQwD`.

System Center Orchestrator

Many existing solutions come with integrated workflow solutions. Think of Microsoft Exchange Server automatically sending an *out of office* notification or of Microsoft SQL Server executing maintenance plans. All these workflow solutions are contained in the product they are part of.

System Center Orchestrator (**SCOR**) is a great addition to Hyper-V and SCSM. Orchestrator provides a workflow management solution for the datacenter. Orchestrator lets you automate the creation, monitoring, and deployment of resources in your environment through workflows known as runbooks. With System SCOR, it is, for instance, possible to span runbooks originating from SCSM to Hyper-V involving, for instance, Microsoft Azure, Microsoft Exchange, and Oracle databases. This greatly simplifies performing daily operations because now you can automate every reoccurring technical process.

Starting with user creation in different systems over VM deployment with automatic backup and restore, up to a fully scripted disaster recovery failover solution, SCOR is capable of building and executing these workflows as follows:

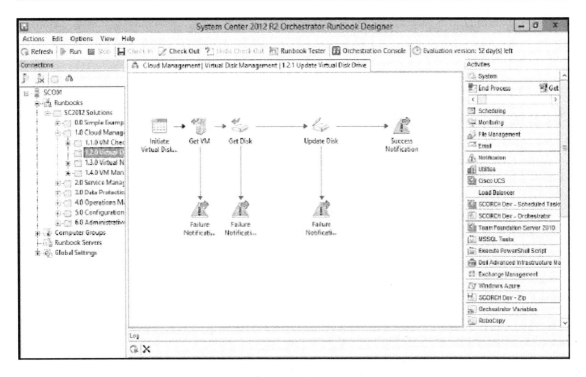

System center orchestrator

Many best practice runbooks around Hyper-V are already built, involving great solutions for automated Hyper-V Replica failover or the creation of machines on Hyper-V with several dependencies. If you have done anything twice in IT, SCOR is the right component to use.

The main steps to get your SCOR installation (described at http://bit.ly/1nh9yQv) up and running are as follows:

1. Download integration packs and add-ons. This is necessary to connect your runbooks to your infrastructure. This configuration is described at http://bit.ly/1nh9Sia.

2. Design your first orchestrator runbook as described in the free e-book at http://bit.ly/1Ch21d3.

For additional information on orchestrator, you can refer to *Microsoft System Center 2012 Orchestrator Cookbook*, by *Samuel Erskine (MCT)*, published by*Packt Publishing*, at `http://bit .ly/1B8tMUY`.

System Center Data Protection Manager

Microsoft's DPM is the bigger version of Windows Server backup (wbadmin) and is itself a complete backup and recovery solution. You can back up Hyper-V clusters on the host level without the need to install backup agents on every virtual machine. You can take consistent backups of running Hyper-V VMs or powered-off virtual machines replicated through Hyper-V Replica. To support the backup of deduplicated volumes, SCDPM is a great backup tool for saving space. SCDPM is also capable of protecting Hyper-V VMs by backing up the replica and not the primary VM. For host-level backups, an SCDPM agent is installed on the Hyper-V host and will protect the entire VM running on that Hyper-V host. For guest-level backup, an SCDPM agent is installed within the VM operating system and is used to protect the workload present within that VM.

SCDPM does not create backups on a classic multirotation principle with frequently occurring full backups. SCDPM uses a more modern approach, creating a single full backup, followed by incremental forever backups every 15 minutes. This removes the classic load-heavy backup window in the middle of the night leading to hours of data loss in a restore. Having recovery available points every 15 minutes offers great point-in-time recovery options, while it's only backing up changed blocks, without the need to rebackup and save the same data over and over again.

It is possible to replicate created backups to another SCDPM server, to a tape device, or to Microsoft Azure. This replaces the need for manual tape rotation and secured offsite transport. The data is stored and transmitted with full encryption.

SCDPM can back up and restore all typical Microsoft workloads in the physical and virtual world, such as Windows Server with Hyper-V:

- Exchange Server
- SQL Server
- SharePoint Server
- Microsoft Dynamics

Remember that Linux VMs running on Hyper-V are also supported Microsoft workloads. In fact, it's easier to run a consistent backup of a Linux system running on Hyper-V than on a physical level. Microsoft has included a **Volume Shadow Copy Service** (**VSS**) for the Linux driver in the Hyper-V integration components for leveraging this capability. SCDPM can protect your Hyper-V environment using SMB shares as well, but this requires the installation of the SCDPM agent on all servers using the SMB remote storage.

SCDPM is supported to perform an **Item-Level Recovery** (**ILR**) of a VM, even if the SCDPM server itself is running as a VM. SCDPM is able to perform an ILR by indexing the VHDs/VHDXs associated with the VM. The SCDPM screen is shown here:

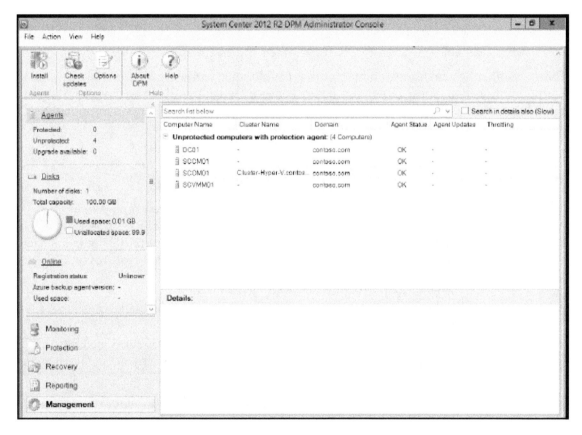

System center data protection manager

After the installation of SCDPM (described at `http://bit.ly/1sTugJj`), follow these steps for a basic configuration:

1. Add SCDPM storage for saving backups. This essential step is described at `http://bit.ly/1tmBhX7`.
2. Install SCDPM protection agents to your Hyper-V hosts and VMs. These agents will communicate to your SCDPM server. The configuration is described at `http://bit.ly/VZkWcu`.
3. Create a Protection Group to configure your backup job. This configuration is described at `http://bit.ly/VZljDK`.

For additional information on SCDPM, you can refer to the book at `http://bit.ly/1rHWKKd`.

There are other System Center components available, such as Configuration Manager and Endpoint Protection. These tools are mostly client-focused and will not be covered in this book; however, they can be utilized for server management as well. Keep in mind that System Center is available for a 180-day trial period, so try it out today.

Automatic System Center deployment

Installing System Center with its various components is a complex and time-consuming task. Microsoft's Rob Willis created the **PowerShell Deployment Toolkit** (**PDT**), which allows the unattended installation of all System Center components within 2 hours instead of spending days manually installing everything. The following are the features of PDT:

- PDT downloads all prerequirements for System Center
- It automatically creates the necessary virtual machines, hosting the System Center installations including operating systems
- It creates the corresponding Active Directory Domain and service accounts
- It installs all System Center prerequirements
- It installs all System Center components of your choice
- It configures basic integration between the installed System Center components

PDT is a great way to create a lab environment quickly for evaluation, but even production setups can be installed through PDT. PDT utilizes XML files for configuration. The required customization of these XML files can be a tricky job. To simplify this process, I have created the PDT GUI together with my coworker, Kamil Kosek.

PDT GUI offers a user interface to edit the XML files necessary for PDT and adds some management improvements for the various PDT components.

PDT and PDT GUI can be downloaded from `http://aka.ms/PDTGUI` and are available for free.

Microsoft Azure

I have discussed some Microsoft Azure solutions that can help to protect your environment in `Chapter 3`, *Backup and Disaster Recovery*. In 2016, a lot of companies are looking for hybrid solutions to protect, automate, and monitor workload in Microsoft Azure. These solutions are included in the Microsoft Operations Management Suite (for further information, check `http://bit.ly/2baW2hs`).

This suite includes several products, which are as follows:

- Azure Site Recovery
- Azure Backup
- Log analytics
- Azure Automation

Azure Site Recovery

As presented in `Chapter 3`, *Backup and Disaster Recovery*, **Azure Site Recovery** (**ASR**) is a solution which enables you to protect your VMs in Microsoft Azure. ASR is also able to protect VMs between two on-premises datacenters by orchestrating the restart of VMs when the failover occurs. The protection in Microsoft Azure is more cost effective, therefore, the focus will be on this solution.

ASR can be part of a business continuity and disaster recovery strategy. ASR can be used either through SCVMM or not, and it is also able to protect physical servers. ASR enables you to replicate the VMs or the physical servers to Microsoft Azure to restart them in Microsoft Azure in the case of disaster:

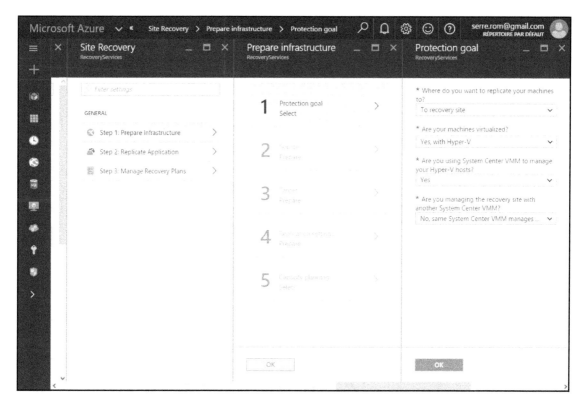

Infrastructure preparation in azure site recovery

The restart of the servers is orchestrated by a recovery plan configured via the Azure Portal. The recovery plan can include a manual task, Microsoft Automation workflow, and a start task. These tasks are sorted in groups to choose the order of execution.

A big advantage of ASR is the opportunity to run a test of failover. In this way, you are able to try your failover in case of disaster and start the VM in azure in a sandbox. When you run a test of failover, the workloads located in the on-premises datacenter are still running.

When you configure ASR, you can map an on-premises network with a Microsoft Azure network. In this way, when a VM failovers to Microsoft Azure, the network is already set.

If you want to implement ASR, be careful about the link between Microsoft Azure and your datacenter. ASR supports site-to-site VPN and ExpressRoute. When you have a large number of workloads to replicate, I recommend that you look for ExpressRoute (for further information, check `http://bit.ly/1OdQylf`).

To use ASR to replicate workloads in Microsoft Azure, you have to follow these main steps:

- Create a Recovery services in Microsoft Azure
- Prepare the infrastructure by installing Azure Site Recovery Agent on the Hyper-V nodes and SCVMM (if you are using it)
- Enable the replication for the VMs
- Create the recovery plan

Azure Backup

Similar to ASR, Azure Backup is a component of Microsoft Azure Recovery Services. This feature enables you to back up a physical server or VMs both on-premises and in Microsoft Azure. Instead of storing your long-term backup in tapes, you can leverage Microsoft Azure. To deploy Azure Backup, you have the following three options:

- Microsoft Azure Backup agent
- System Center Data Protection Manager
- Azure Backup Server

The first option enables you to back up a Windows Server 2008 R2 at least by installing a simple agent. This back up solution can back up files and folders.

You can also leverage SCDPM to store your long-term back up in Microsoft Azure. You just have to install the Azure Backup agent and register the Azure subscription in the SCDPM console. Then, when you configure a protection, you can choose to back up to Microsoft Azure (online protection).

The third solution involves Azure Backup Server. This tool is equivalent to SCDPM except that you can't back up on a tape:

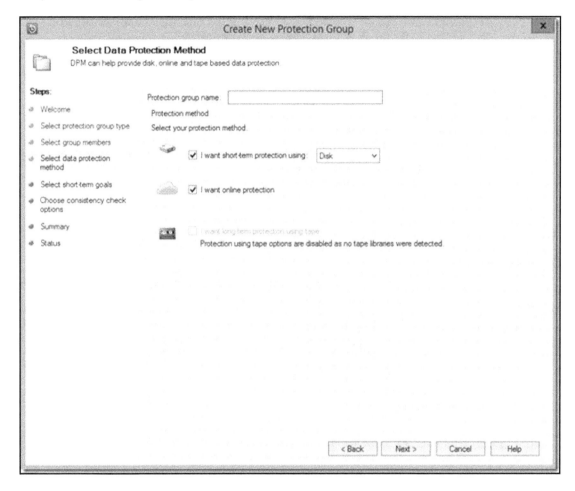

Configure online protection

Either with SCDPM or Azure Backup Server, you can back up Exchange, SharePoint, Windows Server, SQL Server database, and Microsoft Dynamics.

Log Analytics

Log Analytics is a tool that can collect, combine, and correlate data. Then the data can be arranged in a chart for a global overview of your infrastructure. Log Analytics provides a log engine to search information and to create complex requests.

Some solution packs are available through a gallery. A solution pack is a set of rules, visualization, and logic, which provide metrics about a service (such as SQL Server, capacity planning, security, and so on).

Log Analytics can gather information from an agent installed on the servers (either through a gateway or not). Log Analytics can also be connected to SCOM, which will act as a gateway. When you use SCOM, you don't need a further agent-the SCOM agent will be leveraged.

When the servers are connected, data is sent to the Log Analytics workspace to handle it. Then the solution packs deal with data with the log engine to show you information.

For Hyper-V usage, there is a great solution pack called capacity planning. If you have SCVMM and SCOM connected, you can send data to get information about capacity planning:

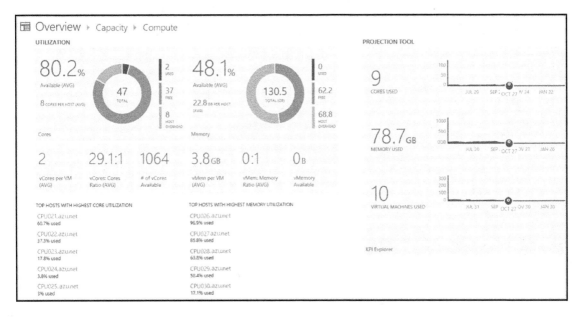

Capacity planning in log analytics

As you can see in the preceding screenshot, Log Analytics gives you information about resource utilization and makes a projection. It is a great tool to have a readable capacity planning.

Log Analytics is also available on mobile devices such as Apple iOS, Google Android, or Windows Mobile. Thanks to the application, you can have the dashboard on your mobile phone.

Azure Automation

When you manage a lot of servers and services, you certainly use PowerShell and/or System Center Orchestrator to automate some tasks. The automation of tasks avoids repeated actions, reduces human errors, and increases the reliability of your IT. Azure Automation enables you to automate tasks in the Cloud or in an on-premises datacenter. Similar to Orchestrator, Azure Automation is based on runbook which can be edited graphically or with the PowerShell command line.

Microsoft has recently added a gallery where you can download runbooks written by the community. For example, you can download runbook to start or stop virtual machines, create a VM, and so on:

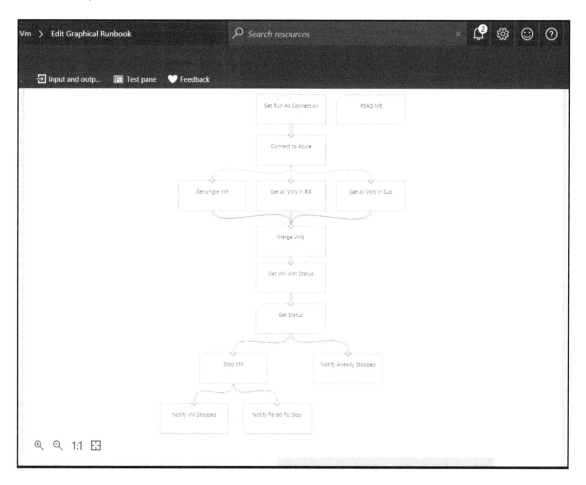

A graphical runbook in azure automation

You can use Azure Automation with ASR to automate some tasks when a failover occurs between your datacenter and Microsoft Azure. For example, you may want to run a diagnostic test during the failover to verify that the service is online before starting other virtual machines.

Summary

Having finished this chapter, you now have an overview of the great capabilities added on top of Hyper-V when running System Center. You can use automatic deployment and operating processes while maintaining great data security through improved backups.

In Chapter 9, *Migration to Hyper-V 2016*, you will learn how to move the existing workloads from physical systems and other hypervisors to Microsoft's virtualization solution, Hyper-V.

A more detailed overview on System Center is available in a free e-book; you can download it from http://bit.ly/1pZQHyj.

9
Migration to Hyper-V 2016

"With the experience of doing several hundred migrations, I have collected some good best practices: do some thorough investigation before moving regarding what is running on those migration objects and preferably do some performance analysis also. After migration from another vendor, do some cleaning of third party software such as VMware tools or raid tools and install the latest VM additions, which can be done automatically."

Niklas Akerlund MVP – Hyper-V

By now, you should be aware of all the important best practices of Hyper-V. To take advantage of all these benefits, it's highly recommended you to use the latest version of Hyper-V-2016. If you are running any older versions of Hyper-V, it is now time to move on. In this chapter, you will learn about the various tools and methods used for upgrading Hyper-V to 2016.

The following topics will be covered in this chapter:

- Export/import/recreation of VMs
- Cross-version live migration
- Copy cluster roles wizard
- Rolling Cluster Upgrade
- Microsoft Virtual Machine Converter (MVMC) and Microsoft Automation Toolkit (MAT)
- Project Shift for MAT and other third-party solutions
- Physical to Virtual (P2V) conversions
- Virtualized domain controllers

Upgrading single Hyper-V hosts

If you are currently running a single host with an older version of Hyper-V and now want to upgrade this host on the same hardware, there is a limited set of decisions to be made. You want to upgrade the host with the least amount of downtime and without losing any data from your virtual machine. Before you start the upgrade process, make sure all components from your infrastructure are compatible with the new version of Hyper-V. Then it's time to prepare your hardware for this new version of Hyper-V by upgrading all firmware to the latest available version and downloading the necessary drivers for Windows Server 2016 with Hyper-V, along with its installation media.

One of the most crucial questions in this update scenario is whether you should use the integrated installation option called **in-place upgrade**, where the existing operating system will be transformed to the recent version of Hyper-V, or delete the current operating system and perform a clean installation.

While the installation experience with in-place upgrades works well when only the Hyper-V role is installed, based on experience, some versions of upgraded systems are more likely to suffer problems. Numbers pulled from the Elanity support database show about 15 percent more support cases on upgraded systems from Windows Server 2008 R2 than clean installations. Remember how fast and easy it is nowadays to do a clean install of Hyper-V; this is why it is highly recommended to do this instead of upgrading existing installations. If you are currently using Windows Server 2012 R2 and want to upgrade to Windows Server 2016, note that we have not yet seen any differences in the number of support cases between the installation methods. However, with clean installations of Hyper-V being so fast and easy, I barely use them.

Before starting any type of upgrade scenario, make sure you have current backups of all affected virtual machines.

Nonetheless, if you want to use the in-place upgrade, insert the Windows Server 2016 installation media and run this command from your current operating system:

```
Setup.exe /auto:upgrade
```

If it fails, it's most likely due to an incompatible application installed on the older operating system. Start the setup without the parameter to find out which applications need to be removed before executing the unattended setup.

If you upgrade from Windows Server 2012 R2, there is no additional preparation needed; if you upgrade from older operating systems, make sure you remove all snapshots from your virtual machines.

Importing virtual machines

If you choose to do a clean installation, you do not necessarily have to export the virtual machines first; just make sure all VMs are powered off and are stored on a different partition from your Hyper-V host OS. If you are using a SAN, disconnect all LUNs before the installation and reconnect them afterwards to ensure their integrity through the installation process. To install the new operating system on the host, just follow the procedures described in Chapter 1, *Accelerating Hyper-V Deployment*. After completing the procedure, just reconnect the LUNs and set the disk online via diskpart or in **Disk Management** at **Control Panel** | **Computer Management**.

If you are using local disks, make sure not to reformat the partition with your virtual machines on it. You should export VM to another location and import them back after reformatting; more efforts are required but it is safer. Set the partition online and then reimport the virtual machines. Before you start the reimport process, make sure all dependencies of your virtual machines are available, especially vSwitches.

To import a single Hyper-V VM, use the following PowerShell cmdlet:

```
Import-VM -Path 'D:\VMs\VM01\Virtual Machines\2D5EECDA-8ECC-4FFC-ACEE-
66DAB72C8754.xml'
```

To import all virtual machines from a specific folder, use this command:

```
Get-ChildItem d:\VMs -Recurse -Filter "Virtual Machines" | %{Get-
ChildItem
    $_.FullName -Filter *.xml} | %{import-vm $_.FullName -Register}
```

After that, all VMs are registered and ready for use on your new Hyper-V hosts. Make sure to update the Hyper-V integration services of all virtual machines before going back into production. If you still have virtual disks in the old .vhd format, it's now time to convert them to .vhdx files. Use this PowerShell cmdlet on powered-off VMs or standalone vDisks to convert a single .vhd file:

```
Convert-VHD -Path d:\VMs\testvhd.vhd -DestinationPath
d:\VMs\testvhdx.vhdx
```

If you want to convert the disks of all your VMs, fellow MVPs, Aidan Finn and Didier van Hoye, have provided a great end-to-end solution to achieve this. This can be found at http://bit.ly/1omOagi.

I often hear from customers that they don't want to upgrade their disks, so as to be able to revert to older versions of Hyper-V when needed. First, you should know that I have never met a customer who has done that because there really is no technical reason why anyone should do this. Second, even if you perform this backwards move, running virtual machines on older Hyper-V hosts is not supported, if they were deployed on more modern versions of Hyper-V before. The reason for this is very simple; Hyper-V does not offer a way to downgrade Hyper-V integration services. The only way to move a virtual machine back to an older Hyper-V host is by restoring a backup of the VM made before the upgrade process.

Exporting virtual machines

If you want to use another physical system running a newer version of Hyper-V, you have multiple possible options. They are as follows:

- When using a SAN as a shared storage, make sure all your virtual machines, including their virtual disks, are located on other LUNs rather than on the host operating system. Disconnect all LUNs hosting virtual machines from the source host and connect them to the target host. Bulk-import the VMs from the specified folders.
- When using SMB3 shared storage from scale-out file servers, make sure to switch access to the shared hosting VMs to the new Hyper-V hosts.
- When using local hard drives and upgrading from Windows Server 2008 SP2 or Windows Server 2008 R2 with Hyper-V, it's necessary to export the virtual machines to a storage location reachable from the new host. Hyper-V servers running legacy versions of the OS (prior to 2012 R2) need to power off the VMs before an export can occur. To export a virtual machine from a host, use the following PowerShell cmdlet:

```
Export-VM -Name VM -Path D:\
```

- To export all virtual machines to a folder underneath the following root, use the following command:

```
Get-VM | Export-VM -Path D:\
```

- In most cases, it is also possible to just copy the virtual machine folders containing virtual hard disks and configuration files to the target location and import them to Windows Server 2016 Hyper-V hosts. However, the export method is more reliable and should be preferred.

- A good alternative for moving virtual machines is to recreate them. If you have another host up-and-running with a recent version of Hyper-V, it may be a good opportunity to also upgrade some guest OSes. For instance, Windows Server 2003 and 2003 R2 have been out of extended support since July 2015. Depending on your applications, it may now be the right choice to create new virtual machines with Windows Server 2016 as a guest operating system and migrate your existing workloads from older VMs to these new machines.

- When using Windows Server 2012 or later, and local hard drives, take a look at the cross-version live migration feature explained next in this chapter.

Cross-version live migration

One of the great improvements in Windows Server 2012 R2 is the ability to move the running virtual machines between hosts that run a different version of Hyper-V in a defined environment. Cross-version live migration simplifies the migration process from Windows Server 2012 to Windows Server 2012 R2 for Hyper-V hosts. In the same way, you can use **Shared-nothing live migration** to move a VM and its storage to another standalone Hyper-V host. While the VM is running, you can now execute a Shared-nothing live migration cross-version. This only works from Windows Server 2012 to its successor Windows Server 2012 R2/2016 and not in any other combination. It also works on clusters. While moving all the storage of the VMs takes a long time, this is the recommended migration option if you want to reduce downtime; there is none, at least at the migration process. You still need to reboot the virtual machines after upgrading the integration services of the guest VMs.

If you are using SMB3 fileshares as storage for your virtual machines, you don't even need to transfer the virtual disks with it, and a cross-version live migration does not take longer than a live migration between the cluster nodes.

Make sure that the source and destination Hyper-V hosts are in the same Active Directory domain or in a trusted domain. This can even be hosted in a different forest. In the case of remote domains, make sure the name resolution is working both ways. Configure vSwitches on the destination hosts to map the source hosts' networks; only then can a successful live migration occur.

Cross-version live migration works the same way as the Shared-nothing live migration you already learned. You can trigger it via PowerShell, Hyper-V Manager, Failover Cluster Manager, or System Center Virtual Machine Manager.

Copy cluster roles wizard

After learning how to upgrade single Hyper-V hosts, let's now take a look at a nice little tool to speed things up when using clustered Hyper-V instances. On Windows Server 2012 and Windows Server 2012 R2, the copy cluster roles wizard, formally known as the **Cluster Migration Wizard**, is available.

With the copy cluster roles wizard, it is possible to move the roles of whole Hyper-V clusters to another Hyper-V cluster, including a cross-version migration of all virtual machines. The copy cluster roles wizard does not initiate cross-version live migration, it requires a manual storage unmap.

The copy cluster roles wizard is primarily used in conjunction with SAN volumes. It connects to the source cluster, copies all vital cluster information such as role configuration, and allows you to just map the storage LUNs from your SAN to your new cluster and start all cluster roles back in a matter of a few seconds. This process is very fast and comfortable; however, it requires a simultaneous downtime for all hosted virtual machines.

You can start the copy cluster roles wizard from the cluster properties at **Failover Cluster Manager**, shown in the following screenshot. I have not seen a PowerShell equivalent yet:

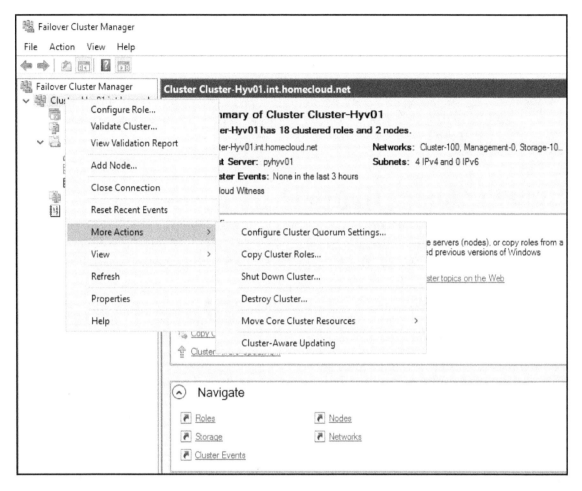

The copy cluster roles Wizard

The first information you need to provide to the copy cluster roles wizard is the name of the old source cluster. The wizard connects to the old cluster and reads in its cluster and role configurations. You will see a list of cluster roles found on the old cluster and ready for migration. Be aware that you can only migrate complete cluster shared volumes with all virtual machines hosted on it. If you are using a traditional one-VM-per-LUN model, you can select individual VMs for migration.

You even have the option to migrate the cluster core roles with their cluster DNS name and IP address. However, this complicates the migration process and is not recommended. Choose unique cluster names and IP addresses for a smooth process.

 If you are still using pass-through disks on your virtual machines, disconnect them before the migration process and convert them afterward to VHDX files. There are some issues with pass-through disk migrations that can be avoided this way.

Rolling cluster upgrade

Since Windows Server 2016, there is a new way to migrate a Windows Server 2012 R2 cluster to Windows Server 2016. This is called **Rolling cluster upgrade**. Now you can mix in the same cluster nodes running on Windows Server 2012 R2 and Windows Server 2016.

Microsoft has implemented a cluster functional level. A cluster running on Windows Server 2012 R2 is at cluster version 8 while a cluster running on Server 2016 is at cluster version 9. When a cluster contains Windows Server 2012 R2 and Windows Server 2016 nodes, it is in mixed OS mode but still in cluster version 8.

To upgrade the cluster, you have to evict each node one by one. When a node is evicted, you have to upgrade the node to Windows Server 2016 (I recommend that you do a clean install). Once the node is in Windows Server 2016, you can add it again to the cluster:

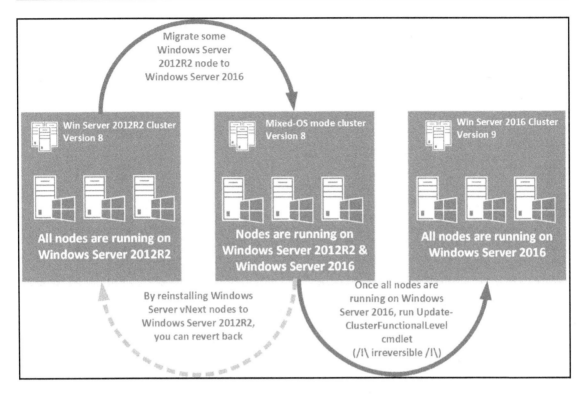

Rolling Cluster Upgrade

Once all cluster nodes are upgraded to Windows Server 2016, you can run this PowerShell cmdlet:

```
Update-ClusterFunctionalLevel
```

I don't recommend that you stay for a long time in the mixed OS mode state. This state exists for a short time and for the migration duration. Moreover, once the cluster is in the Mixed-OS mode state, you have to use the new Failover Clustering Manager console provided by Windows Server 2016.

Migrating VMware virtual machines

If you are running virtual machines on VMware ESXi hosts, there are really good options available for moving them to Hyper-V. There are different approaches on how to convert a VMware virtual machine to Hyper-V: from the inside of the VM on a guest level, running cold conversions with the VM powered off; on the host level, running hot conversions on a running VM; and so on. I will give you a short overview of the currently available tools in the market.

System Center VMM

You have already seen the System Center VMM in earlier chapters for fabric and cloud management. SCVMM can also be used for a limited set of **Virtual to Virtual** (**V2V**) conversions of its VMs. SCVMM V2V functions don't have any recent updates and are prone to errors. SCVMM should not be the first tool of your choice, take a look at MVMC combined with MAT to get equal functionality from a better working tool.

The earlier versions of SCVMM allowed online or offline conversions of VMs; the current version, 2016, allows only offline conversions of VMs. Select a powered-off VM on a VMware host or from the SCVMM library share to start the conversion. The VM conversion will convert VMware-hosted virtual machines through vCenter and ensure that the entire configuration, such as memory, virtual processor, and other machine configurations, is also migrated from the initial source. The tool also adds virtual NICs to the deployed virtual machine on Hyper-V.

The VMware tools must be uninstalled before the conversion because you won't be able to remove the VMware tools when the VM is not running on a VMware host. SCVMM 2016 supports ESXi hosts running 4.1 and 5.1 but not the latest ESX Version 5.5. SCVMM conversions are great to automate through their integrated PowerShell support and it's very easy to install upgraded Hyper-V integration services as part of the setup or by adding any kind of automation through PowerShell or System Center Orchestrator. Besides manually removing VMware tools, using SCVMM is an end-to-end solution in the migration process. You can find some PowerShell examples for SCVMM-powered V2V conversion scripts at `http://bit.ly/Y4bGp8`.

I no longer recommend the use of this tool because Microsoft now spends no time on it.

Microsoft Virtual Machine Converter

Microsoft released its first version of the free solution accelerator **Microsoft Virtual Machine Converter** (**MVMC**) in 2013, and it should be available in Version 3.1 by the release of this book. MVMC provides a small and easy option to migrate selected virtual machines to Hyper-V. It takes a very similar approach to the conversion as SCVMM does. The conversion happens at a host level and offers a fully integrated end-to-end solution. MVMC supports all recent versions of VMware vSphere. It will even uninstall the VMware tools and install the Hyper-V integration services. MVMC 2.0 works with all supported Hyper-V guest operating systems, including Linux.

MVMC comes with a full GUI wizard as well as a fully scriptable **command-line interface** (**CLI**). Besides being a free tool, it is fully supported by Microsoft in the event you experience any problems during the migration process. MVMC should be the first tool of your choice if you do not know which tool to use. Like most other conversion tools, it does the actual conversion on the MVMC server itself and requires its disk space to host the original VMware virtual disk as well as the converted Hyper-V disk. MVMC even offers an add-on for VMware virtual center servers to start conversions directly from the vSphere console.

The current release of MV is freely available at its official download site at `http://bit.ly/1HbRIg7`.

Download MVMC to the conversion system and start the click-through setup. After finishing the download, start the MVMC with the GUI by executing `Mvmc.Gui.exe`. The wizard guides you through some choices.

MVMC is not only capable of migrating to Hyper-V but also allows you to move virtual machines to Microsoft Azure. Follow these few steps to convert a VMware VM:

1. Select Hyper-V as a target.
2. Enter the name of the Hyper-V host you want this VM to run on and specify a fileshare to use and the format of the disks you want to create. Choosing the **dynamically expanding** disk feature should be the best option most of the time.
3. Enter the name of the ESXi server you want to use as a source as well as valid credentials.
4. Select the virtual machine to convert. Make sure it has VMware tools installed. The VM can be either powered on or off.
5. Enter a workspace folder to store the converted disk.
6. Wait for the process to finish.

There is some additional guidance available at `http://bit.ly/1vBqj0U`.

This is a great and easy way to migrate a single virtual machine. Repeat the steps for every other virtual machine you have, or use some automation.

Microsoft Automation Toolkit

If you have a number of virtual machines to convert, the **Microsoft Automation Toolkit** (**MAT**) is a great choice. It adds a layer of automation above MVMC and can be downloaded from `http://bit.ly/XyLgeG`.

MAT is a collection of PowerShell scripts that automate conversions using the MVMC. It's backended by the current versions of a SQL Server (SQL Express will work). You can use it to convert several machines at once on a single server or across many servers. The automation options of MAT can be extended to a fully customized end-to-end solution. However, even in a fully automated environment, the conversion will take a lot of time. All virtual disks must be converted in a V2V conversion by all common tools. This takes time on a single virtual disk and a lot of time on multiple virtual disks. The time directly correlates to the size of the virtual disks as well.

Some additional guidance on MAT can be found at `http://bit.ly/1B8tSf5`.

There is one solution available to speed up the conversion process, which we will discuss in the next section.

MAT powered by Project Shift

If you think of MAT as an add-on for MVMC, then MAT powered by Project Shift is another add-on on top of that. Project Shift enables hardware-accelerated conversions of virtual disks. It converts virtual disks located on a NetApp storage controller between formats at amazing speeds. It can convert between several formats, but the most interesting is the VMDK to VHD conversion. For example, I was able to convert a 40 GB VMDK to a VHDX using the following PowerShell cmdlet:

```
ConvertTo-NaVhd
```

This conversion took about 6 seconds. As of today, this only works on the NetApp storage controller because the NetApp controller simply repoints the data from the VMDK into a Hyper-V VHD, writing the appropriate metadata as it progresses. The resulting file is a VHD or VHDX file that takes up practically no extra space on disk and is finished in seconds. While NetApp Shift is available on a NetApp filer, it does not allow for whole VM conversions. This is why Microsoft combined it with MAT to build-again-an end-to-end conversion experience.

MAT powered by Project Shift scales extremely well and is the first choice of tool for a migration for hundreds of virtual machines. It is so successful that I have seen customers running other storage systems borrowing the NetApp filer to leverage these hardware-assisted conversions. Some additional guidance can be found at `http://bit.ly/1tRiMcc`.

Other V2V scenarios

There are a bunch of other tools available in the market for V2V conversions. The 5nine V2V easy converter and the StarWind V2V converter offer a very similar experience to that of the MVMC + MAT solution accelerators but can add particular value needed in advanced migration scenarios.

There is one tool in particular that can add real value to the shown conversion scenarios. The **Double-take Move** by Vision Solution offers a lot more out-of-the-box automation options, such as integration with System Center Orchestrator and Service Manager, and it comes with superior capabilities, such as replicating running VMware VMs to Hyper-V. However, it comes with a price—literally. It is not free and requires a license per migrated virtual machine. Use Double-take Move if money is not your most valuable resource and you are looking for a fully automated conversion experience.

All mentioned tools are focused on moving from VMware to Hyper-V. What if you have virtual machines running on Citrix XenServer?

Citrix offers a free tool called **XenConvert**, which is available at `http://bit.ly/WXrnhd`, and it allows for the conversion of XenServer VMs into the OVF format. The OVF format is just a container format hosting the XenServer VM configuration and its virtual hard drive in a VHD format. This conversion can be done with the following steps:

1. Create a new virtual machine in Hyper-V.
2. Attach the VHD file found in the OVF container.
3. Boot up the virtual machine.
4. Upgrade its integration services and you are done with the conversion.

Some additional guidance can be found at `http://marcusdaniels.net/quick-and-easy-x enserver-to-hyper-v-conversion/`.

If you have virtual machines running on any other Hypervisor than vSphere or Citrix, treat the VM the same way you would treat physical server systems.

Physical to Virtual conversions

While server virtualization is common in Enterprise datacenter, most of my customers are still running some physical server systems for legacy reasons. Those workloads can be transferred to virtual machines as well with **Physical to Virtual** (**P2V**) conversions.

Again, there are several tools available on the market to accomplish this task, including the new MVMC 3.0, SCVMM 2012 SP1 (the R2 version dropped P2V support in favor of MVMC 3.0), and Disc2VHD. P2V conversions are very complex tasks.

Disc2VHD is started on the physical system you want to convert. Stop all databases and services involved in your server workloads and let Disc2VHD do its work. It will create a VSS snapshot and then create a VHDX file on a per-block level from the physical disk and its partition. Just attach this created VHDX file, which is bootable, to a newly created Hyper-V VM. This is very simple but most efficient.

This is shown in the following screenshot:

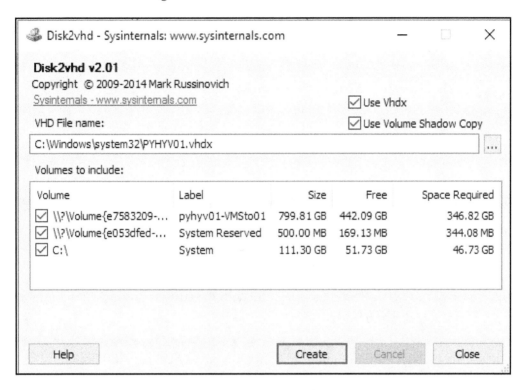

Disc2VHD

Like most P2V solutions, there is some cleaning to be done afterward to remove old physical drivers from the system. While I highly recommend removing network and local printer drivers from the VM, I have not seen any harm done by any other kind of a driver.

To remove a driver from a device no longer connected to the system, a special view of **Device Manager** is necessary. Open a command prompt as administrator and run the following commands:

```
set DEVMGR_SHOW_NONPRESENT_DEVICES=1
devmgmt.msc
```

A **Device Manager** window opens. Navigate to **View** | **Show hidden devices** | **Network adapters**, right-click on any grayed-out items, and select **Uninstall**. Repeat the same process for a local printer if installed and make sure to reboot the system afterward. Your system is now production-ready. Some additional guidance can be found at `http://bit.ly/1mbMfK j`.

There are no experiences yet with MVMC 3.0, as it was only released around the same time as this book.

Virtualizing domain controllers

The last best practice I want to give you is about moving special workloads to Hyper-V. After having done many P2V migrations, there are only two workloads that deserve the attribute *special*: a small business server and a domain controller. The first one is very simple—don't try to convert small business servers, they are outdated. Create a new virtual machine and rebuild the services offered by SBS with the current products. If you get rid of the SBS server in the process, every IT person will love you.

The second one deserves special consideration. Is it a good idea to virtualize domain controllers? Absolutely, they are built for it. Should you convert physical domain controllers? If you have to, you can do it. Often, it is faster to just deploy a new DC to the existing domain and remove the old one after that from the domain.

Should you virtualize all your domain controllers? Absolutely not. Domain controllers run great in virtual machines; however, due to problems related to time synchronization and a chicken and egg problem related to Hyper-V hosts hosting their own DCs, you should still place one physical domain controller for each domain. Another reason to not virtualize all DCs is to do with the Hyper-V cluster. To start the cluster, a DC must be alive. If all DCs are virtualized in the cluster, no DC is available and the cluster can't start. While it is absolutely possible to overcome this limitation and virtualize the last domain controller too, it's often not worth the hassle and therefore not the best practice.

Additional information on this topic can be found at `http://bit.ly/1q06ygi`.

Summary

Having finished this book with this last chapter, you have read a lot about Hyper-V best practices. You learned about faster Hyper-V deployment, HA options, and disaster recovery scenarios. You saw the most relevant best practices around storage, network, and performance tuning. You read overviews about central management with System Center for Hyper-V and, last but not least, you know how to move the existing services to Hyper-V.

All this can only lead to one conclusion: your Hyper-V skills are now ready for production!

Index

www.ingramcontent.com/pod-product-compliance
Lightning Source LLC
LaVergne TN
LVHW081339050326
832903LV00024B/1221